Jack Wattley's
Handbook of Discus

A young turquoise discus bred by the author. This is the usual selling size at which the colors of the fish can be guaranteed.

Front & Back Cover Photos by Hans Georg Petersmann

Distributed in the UNITED STATES by T.F.H. Publications, Inc., 211 West Sylvania Avenue, Neptune City, NJ 07753; in CANADA by H & L Pet Supplies Inc., 27 Kingston Crescent, Kitchener, Ontario N2B 2T6; Rolf C. Hagen Ltd., 3225 Sartelon Street, Montreal 382 Quebec; in ENGLAND by T.F.H. Publications Limited, 4 Kier Park, Ascot, Berkshire SL5 7DS; in AUSTRALIA AND THE SOUTH PACIFIC by T.F.H. (Australia) Pty. Ltd., Box 149 Brookvale 2100 N.S.W., Australia; in NEW ZEALAND by Ross Haines & Son, Ltd., 18 Monmouth Street, Grey Lynn, Auckland 2 New Zealand; in SINGAPORE AND MALAYSIA by MPH Distributors (S) Pte., Ltd., 601 Sims Drive, # 03/07/21, Singapore 1438; in the PHILIPPINES by Bio-Research, 5 Lippay Street, San Lorenzo Village, Makati Rizal; in SOUTH AFRICA by Multipet Pty. Ltd., 30 Turners Avenue, Durban 4001. Published by T.F.H. Publications Inc., Ltd. the British Crown Colony of Hong Kong.

TABLE OF CONTENTS

CAPTION FOR PAGE 4
A map of South America that will assist you in locating the areas where Jack Wattley found his discus. Map courtesy of the Hammond Map Corp.

CAPTION FOR PAGE 5
The four photographs show Jack Wattley . . . the dreamer whose dreams came true . . . surrounded by his own creations. Wattley's intent is to develop a strain of discus completely covered with metallic turquoise. As you can see from the fish shown in the photos on page 5, he is coming closer and closer to his final objective. Photos by Dr. Herbert R. Axelrod.

Jack Wattley's Handbook of Discus

Foreword

Jack Wattley, 61 years old, of English and French descent, was born in Cleveland, Ohio, and now lives in Fort Lauderdale, Florida.

For over 20 years, he has occupied himself with the study of the species and subspecies of the genus *Symphysodon*—the discus fishes. Because of the splendor of their coloration and their odd shape, they are considered the most beautiful freshwater fishes. Their care and especially their breeding confronts aquarists with problems which often are difficult to solve.

As early as 1962, Jack Wattley caught the first discus in Lake Tefe and later the pale-blue striped giant discus in the Rio Jurua (Brazil). In Colombia and Peru, he collected varicolored specimens of *Symphysodon aequifasciata.*

Mr. Wattley attained international recognition with his green-striped discus fish, which he named the turquoise discus. By a systematic selection among hundreds of offspring of the fish captured in the wild, he obtained fish with a regular green lengthwise stripe pattern and bright colors, such as occur only rarely in nature. In the region of the Amazon River, the discus do not select their partners according to the beauty ideals of aquarists. Among hundreds of fish caught in the wild, only a few nicely striped discus are found.

Discus pairs kept under less than optimal conditions and weakened by illness and medication will often eat their offspring; Dr. Rolf Geisler described a pair that ate their spawn 30 times. The parent animals often transfer parasites to their young, which may lead to the death of the delicate animals. For these reasons, Jack Wattley raises his young fish artificially. After many years of painstaking experiments he now succeeds in raising 90% of the young fish artificially.

In order to pass on his experience and to broaden his own knowledge, Mr. Wattley travelled through many countries, including Japan, Malaysia, Taiwan, Hong Kong, Thailand, and Canada, where he visited the best-known discus breeders. He visits Western Germany every year.

In the pages that follow, Jack Wattley describes his impressions of his travels and gives advice on the care and breeding of discus. He treats the water conditions, the breeding, the feeding and the capture of wild fish.

Discus fanciers are grateful to Jack Wattley for passing on his experiences. They will help prevent losses and maintain our enjoyment of our hobby.

Dr. Eduard Schmidt-Focke
January, 1985

Introduction

As I stand on the soft, damp floor of the Brazilian rain forest, I can see but a very small part of the life of the jungle. Forty feet overhead the moss-covered trunks of the trees merge into a solid canopy of green foliage. Almost immediately I see several morpho butterflies with large iridescent blue wings that glitter in the subdued light. In a flash the many weeks of preparation for this trip roll before my eyes, climaxing on the moment of my arrival in the tiny Amazon town of Leticia, Colombia, a jumping-off spot for any tropical fish collecting in Colombia, Peru, or western Brazil. The pilot of a small private airplane who will fly me into Brazil and back to Leticia is contacted. Several hours later and two hundred miles east of Leticia, I find myself in Carauari, Brazil, on the Rio Jurua. Here I am at last in the Brazilian Amazon, home of the discus, *Symphysodon.*

A local fisherman is found, one Luis da Silva, who knows the small discus streams and lakes from Carauari to Curimata, a distance of approximately 15 miles. This is the dry season. The feeder streams, lakes, and lagoons are low, with discus areas being no more than 2 feet deep. The water is clear, and the bottoms of the streams are sandy. The water temperature is in the mid-70's Fahrenheit, for with such heavy vegetation overhead practically no sunlight enters these tiny streams and the water simply cannot warm up.

We string the fishing seine across the 10-foot stream and wait for Luis's two companions to flush the discus out from the crevices and coves that line the shallow shoreline. They begin to poke with wooden poles about 30 to 40 feet from us. Finally, the discus appear! Some avoid the seine, but others dash wildly into the netting.

We begin to sort out the discus, and to my dismay my guides throw the small discus with no color into the bushes along the banks to die, showing no consideration for the conservation of native wildlife. I try to explain to them why they must not throw the small ones away and then proceed with gentle care to take all of the brightly colored ones while wondering how many of these beautiful jewels will ultimately find their way back alive to my tanks in the United States. It is interesting to note that the great majority of the discus we catch are simply brown in color and that the large specimens are quickly claimed by the natives to end up in their cooking pans.

The night is spent in a *maloca,* or native hut, where I attempt to sleep in a tiny, worn-out hammock. During the night I see what looks like a large moth land from time to time on the netting covering my hammock. When the "moth" begins to crawl on the top of the netting I start to crawl out of the hammock. Luis is alarmed. What am I doing for him to show such alarm? He points to the creature. It is not a moth, it is a small vampire bat! We knock it down to the floor and kill it. I kick the bat into a corner of the *maloca,* but the following morning when I look for the animal in order to examine it closely, it is gone. The next three days are not spent catching discus, for I am too sick with fever and diarrhea.

Finally, I go back to Leticia and on to Iquitos, Peru. Several days later, guarding my valuable discus as though they were gold, I hitch a ride on a cargo plane flying directly to Miami, Florida, except for one scheduled stop in Maracaibo, Venezuela, to pick up frozen cocktail shrimp.

These few Carauari discus, along with discus I caught near Tefe, Amazonas, Brazil, will enable me to begin the development of the renowned Wattley turquoise discus. The real challenge is ahead!

Jack Wattley

1

3

2

1. Dr. Eduard Schmidt-Focke (left) and Jack Wattley in the discus room of Dr. Schmidt's home near Frankfurt, Germany.
2. Jack Wattley and Mitsuru Hirose. Hirose-san is the best known discus breeder in Japan. This meeting took place in Nara-shino, Japan.
3. From left to right: Mrs. Seigfried Homann, Jack Wattley, and Dr. Eduard Schmidt-Focke.
4. Wattley's turquoise discus, male below, female above. Photo by Dr. Joseph Jagust.

CAPTIONS FOR PAGE 9
1. A Wattley turquoise discus. Photo by Wattley.
2. A young pair of Wattley turquoise discus.
3. A male *Symphysodon aequifasciata haraldi* imported directly from Singapore.

4

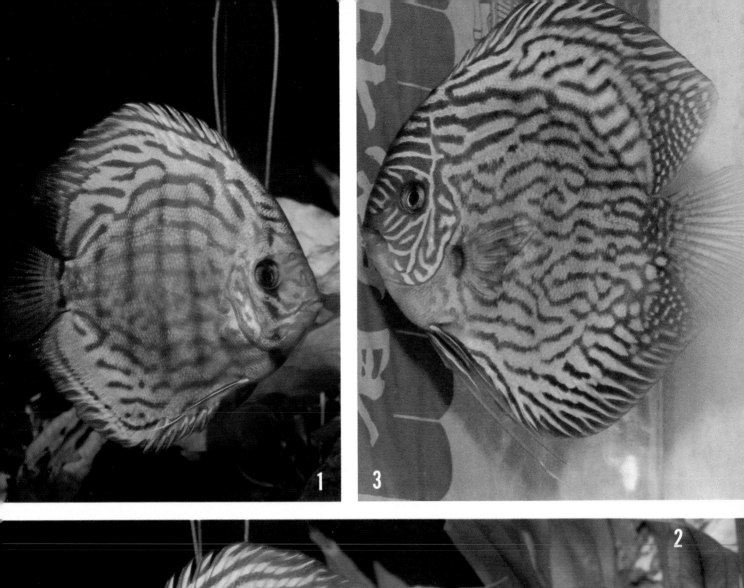

Jack Wattley's Handbook of Discus

The discus belongs to the genus *Symphysodon* of the family Cichlidae. Initially described in 1840 by Dr. Johann Jacob Heckel of Vienna, Austria, the discus made its first appearance in the aquarium trade in the early 1930's both in the United States and Germany. The fish was initially given the trade name of pompadour fish. What was seen by these few privileged early aquarists was the brown discus that would later be named *Symphysodon aequifasciata axelrodi*.

There were attempted spawnings at that time in both countries, with some limited success. Undoubtedly the early failures to successfully maintain the fish were due to improper water temperature as well as the almost total lack of water changes. I seriously doubt that incorrect feeding of the discus contributed to the slow and minimal progress achieved. Live food in the 1930's and 1940's was certainly regarded as more important than it is now. *Daphnia* (water fleas), *Enchytraeus albidus* (whiteworms), *Lumbricus terrestris* (earthworms), and mosquito larvae (usually *Culex pipiens*) were readily available and popular as foods for most tropical fishes.

There was also serious doubt that discus of both sexes were being made available to the public. This criticism was also made concerning the first all-black *Pterophyllum scalare* (angelfish) that arrived in the United States from Hong Kong. These Oriental tank-raised angelfish rarely spawned; but this was not because of the availability of just one sex but because as in the case of the discus they had not been properly conditioned for eventual spawning.

After World War II many more discus began to appear due to more efficient methods of shipping all tropical fishes. Regular water changes were also becoming recognized as important, and no fish benefited more from these water changes than the discus.

An advantage that the discus fancier had at that time was the availability of clean live food. Flaked food in "Madison Avenue" packaging was not yet preponderant and freeze-dried food was not available. Advanced fish keepers did recognize the importance of food such as the Gordon's Formula, but the average hobbyist basically had at his disposal only live foods or poorly prepared dried foods in small one-ounce cans. Neither live tubificid worms (for better or for worse) nor live brine shrimp were readily available.

Bits of successful discus information began to appear in international aquarium literature in the late 1950's and early 1960's. At that same time tropical fish collecting centers such as Iquitos, Peru; Leticia, Colombia; and Manaus and Belem do Para, Brazil, became more accessible to limited air travel, and much larger quantities of discus began to appear on the market.

Likewise, discus collectors in South America were rapidly learning new methods of capturing the discus. With the increase in air traffic and improved flight schedules the discus began to arrive in both Europe and the United States in relatively good condition. It was entirely possible for a discus to reach a tropical fish dealer's tank in Frankfurt, West Germany, or New York City just three or four days after being caught in a jungle stream. Neither the fishermen nor the South American exporters made any attempt to feed the discus. Feeding was unnecessary in many instances because the fish would arrive at their point of destination in a short period of time due to the improved flight schedules.

By the autumn of 1962, not only *Symphysodon aequifasciata axelrodi* (brown discus) were arriving in Miami and New York City, but also fairly large quantities of *Symphysodon discus* (Heckel's discus). Very limited numbers of *Symphysodon aequifasciata aequifasciata* (Peruvian green discus) as well as *Symphysodon aequifasciata haraldi* (blue discus) were beginning to make more regular appearances.

At this time many of the arriving Heckel's discus were being sold as blue discus because some of the tropical fish importers were not aware of any differences between the two species. A rumor circulated among several of the importers in the Miami area that these

Background of the Discus

arriving Heckel's discus were being caught in small streams in Guyana. To say the least, this was not the case. The fish were simply being air-shipped from Manaus, Amazonas, Brazil, to Guyana.

Today, discus are available as never before and are no longer considered a rarity. Discus are financially within the reach of the interested hobbyist, and the aquarium shop that does not stock the fish is, indeed, an exception.

Amazonia, encompassing parts of Venezuela, Colombia, Brazil, and Peru, is the home of the discus. This vast territory has interconnected waterways during the rainy season, thereby joining many rivers, lakes, and streams. This is the reason discus can be found in most of the smaller Amazonian waters. I doubt that discus could thrive for long in the major rivers such as the Putumayo, Negro, Tapajos, and Madeira. During the months of high water the major rivers spill out over their banks, inundating vast areas of the jungle. It is very probable that these high-water rivers are highways of dispersal over which discus can pass from one river system to the other, thus allowing for interbreeding and genetic interchange.

The heavy rains begin in earnest in most parts of the Amazon region in December, but the rivers do not begin to rise to any great degree until January or February. By May or June the principal rivers are approximately 40 feet higher than during the months of October or November, with the exception of the Rio Negro, which is a Northern Hemisphere river that has not even reached high water by June. Thus, the collecting of discus is most difficult and uncomfortable during most of the year, with the exception of the months of October and November. I completed all of my discus collecting during the months of October, November, and early December, when the rains that gather over the distant Andes mountains are quite infrequent. Naturally, this makes a discus-collecting venture a bit more logical. I have received numerous requests for precise information about the best time of the year to collect discus in South America. However, giving advice on the level of the rivers is like trying to prophesy whether it will rain at a certain time in some distant Andean village. These conditions are both dependent on the winds over the Andes.

During my third trip to the Amazon water analyses were made in several locations in streams north of the Putumayo River near the Colombian-Brazilian border. The results (averages) were as follows:

pH—6.6
hardness—25 ppm
iron—1.7 ppm
alkalinity—20 ppm
chlorides—3.0 ppm

A conductivity meter to measure the total dissolved solids was not available at that time, but it is common knowledge that the water will average approximately 10 ppm total dissolved solids.

CAPTIONS FOR PAGE 12
1. Dr. Eduard Schmidt-Focke before his marriage to Miss Focke. He took her family name as part of his in order to preserve it, as she was the last living person in the family with that name.
2. The German turquoise discus raised by Dr. Schmidt.
3. One of Dr. Schmidt's first experiments produced this cross between *Symphysodon aequifasciata haraldi* and *S. a. aequifasciata*.
4. A Bangkok red discus, one of the color strains originated by Dr. Schmidt. Photo by Lo Wing Yat.
5. A Hong Kong blue discus.

CAPTION FOR PAGE 13
Dr. Eduard Schmidt-Focke originated more color strains of discus than any other person. He was a close personal friend of the late Harald Schultz and of Dr. Herbert R. Axelrod, and they gave him colorful specimens they collected all over Brazil. It was from these specimens that he developed this female red turquoise discus. The term "turquoise" is, however, a term usually restricted to Wattley's turquoise. Photo by Klaus Schmidt.

Great amounts of organic matter, for the most part humus, are taken from the jungle floor and with the help of the heavy rains enter the rivers and streams, thereby creating the well-known "black water" of Amazonia. It is very interesting to note that there are three distinct types of Amazon waters: black water, known as *agua preta* in Brazil; clear water; and white water, which is known as *agua branca* in Brazil.

Clean black water looks exactly like strong coffee or tea—very clear and dark in color. As previously stated, this coloring is due for the most part to humic acids that leach into the river waters during the rainy season. I found very little aquatic life in these black waters with the exception of some small and nondescript tetras (characins). An average pH reading was found to be 4.2 to 4.8, thus making it too acidic to support insects or fishes to any degree.

The clear water is found in most instances in the small feeder streams that become virtually isolated from the main bodies of water during the dry season when all the Amazonian waters recede to their lowest points. These tiny streams generally have sandy bottoms and the currents are quite strong, a point that was proved when the author placed a floating aquarium thermometer in the water and it was swept away in a matter of seconds.

The *agua branca* or white water is a mixture of several waters: clear, black and muddy. In many discus collecting areas the so-called white water looks very much like the Mississippi River in the United States, turbid and beige or light tan rather than white in color. The mineral content of the white water is higher than that in the black water streams; the pH is between 6.0 and 7.0. As with all Amazonian waters (which have virtually no sodium, iron, calcium, or magnesium), the collector can be assured that the total hardness will be very low.

It is in these waters that discus are found. During the dry season they will be in the little shallow brooks and streams. Needless to say, it is much easier to capture them at this time of the year.

Any collecting location will most likely be far removed from towns and villages. The collector would be wise to seek the expert help and advice of native fishermen from the local area. Usually the collector has to travel in a small wooden boat with an outboard motor of 25 horsepower to the *igarapes* or discus streams; this can also entail an overland hike of at least several hours through the jungle. Tiny, fast-flowing brooks are crossed until the isolated discus stream is found. The water depth is shallow, generally not more than 2 feet. If the little stream harboring the discus is in a very dense part of the jungle, the water temperature will be approximately 72°F. This is due to the fact that the sun's rays never penetrate the dense foliage to warm the water to the normal Amazonian temperature of approximately 85 to 87°F. I found discus in these isolated streams that were harboring eye abscesses and fin and body fungus. This was due, no doubt, to the very cool waters.

The native fishermen know the natural habitat of the discus. When a good location is reached several of the fishermen will immediately jump into the shallow stream, poking and jabbing with long wooden poles into the caves and holes that line the stream banks. This activity is meant to flush out any discus that may be hiding in that area. Approximately 25 feet downstream from where the two or three natives are trying to frighten out the discus, two or three more fishermen will have a nylon seine or cast net strung completely across the stream. If the discus are driven out from their hiding places they will generally dash rapidly *en masse* directly into the seine. At this point confusion reigns, with some of the discus slipping under or around the netting, some jumping over the net, and some simply backing off and swimming wildly back to the protective cover of the caves. The experience and agility of the fishermen come to the fore, and the majority of the discus school will be quickly encompassed by the netting and captured.

Once the discus are securely in the seine their days of freedom are over. At this point they will take one of three possible "routes." If they are of interest to the collector, they will be claimed by him. If they are not of interest to the collector and are not undersized, they will be taken by the fishermen and will end up on their dining tables. If the fish are undersized they will have the inglorious ending of being tossed up into the underbrush to die a slow death, for no wildlife conservation is practiced here.

The discus claimed by the collector will be put immediately into plastic bags and carried back to town. Many stops are made along the way to change the discus' water. Once in town the collector has to make a decision about how to house the discus until departure time. I have always chosen to house the discus in floating enclosures of soft netting directly in the lake areas near the encampments where I was staying. Since the discus have experienced a traumatic environmental change, no attempt is made to feed them at this point or at any other time until they reach their final destination.

Another method of catching discus in the Amazon is by fishing directly from a boat at night. I participated in this type of nighttime discus fishing once with absolutely no luck. Nevertheless, this method is used by most discus fishermen, and they do achieve good results.

In the case of nighttime fishing from a small boat, each fishermen is equipped with a sturdy hand net and a flashlight fastened securely to a head brace, thus allowing the native the full use of both hands. The small fishing boat very quietly and smoothly patrols the shoreline of the small lake or lagoon, with the occupants continually looking in the logical places for the discus, which are called *pelecos* by most of the Brazilian fishermen. The protective cover afforded the discus will be a fallen tree or the submerged roots and branches of trees lining the shoreline. The very brief "blindness" of the discus, caused by shining the flashlight directly at it, allows the fishermen a few seconds to gently slip his dip net under the fish to capture it. A successful night's fishing can result in the capture of several dozen discus.

Although discus can be found to a greater or lesser extent in most regions of the Amazon, it is very difficult to state exactly where each color variety abounds. Manaus, Amazonas, Brazil, can be considered as the point of origin for collecting trips. Starting from Manaus and proceeding in an easterly direction to Belem, Para, Brazil, the overwhelming majority of the discus found will be of the common brown variety, *Symphysodon aequifasciata axelrodi*. These discus range in background color from medium brown to brown/gray. They are found in most of the feeder streams leading to the principal rivers of the Rio Urubu, Rio Tapajos, and the Rio Tocantins.

The Rio Tocantins is an extremely interesting river and is only a two-day boat trip from Belem. Fishing the small lagoons and lakes near the Tocantins will most likely reward the fisherman with a catch of brown discus. However, there is probably no better area for collecting brown discus than near Santarem, Para, Brazil, located 480 river miles east of Manaus. This area is situated at the mouth of the Rio Tapajos where the darkened waters (green in color) meet the muddy Amazon. The line of demarcation of the waters is more clearly defined here than at Manaus. The Tapajos is like an island sea, being 15 miles wide near its mouth. By taking a boat directly from Santarem the fisherman can penetrate the small, narrow tributaries that for mystical beauty are unequaled anywhere in Amazonia. It is also in these tiny lakes and lagoons that the brown discus can be found.

CAPTIONS FOR PAGE 16
1. This *Symphysodon a. aequifasciata* was collected in Tefe, Brazil, by Dr. Axelrod and was given to Dr. Schmidt-Focke. Using fish like this one but greener, he developed the magnificent green discus shown by the two examples (#2). Photo #1 by Dr. Axelrod; photo #2 by A. L. Pieter.
3. These are *Symphysodon d. discus* originally described by Heckel and therefore called "discus Heckel." Wattley raises these fish, too.

CAPTIONS FOR PAGE 17
1. A Wattley royal blue discus, one of the strains for which Wattley is famous.
2. A group of young Wattley turquoise discus. Wattley built his fame and fortune by breeding fancy discus when other breeders were happy to breed any kind of discus.

I traveled 75 miles northwest from Santarem to a lake region off the mainstream of the Amazon looking for exotic discus and found nothing interesting. Even the little area "trading post" of Oriximina was uninteresting. Nevertheless, *Symphysodon discus* Heckel has been found a bit further to the northwest on the Trombetas River.

Starting from Manaus again and traveling in a westerly/northwesterly direction, the collector will encounter the much more brilliantly colored discus. To the northwest, up the Rio Negro from Manaus, the river life is utterly absorbing and a photographic gold mine of log booms, dugout canoes, passenger-cargo ships, banana boats, police boats, children and even chickens swimming, waterside huts on stilts, and squat river launches that carry produce, horses, cattle, and people up and down the river. When the hurly-burly, kaleidoscopic color of the floating market is added to the scene, the picture is complete. Needless to say, these sights are infrequent, but they are there and they are vivid. Seen near the small streams are brilliantly colored butterflies, parrots, huge banyan trees, and spreading kapok trees. During the months of June, July and August the queenly *Victoria regia* lilies with pads up to 6 feet in diameter show their white or dark pink blooms.

This general area in the Brazilian state of Amazonas is the home of *Symphysodon discus* Heckel. This species will not be found in the black waters of the Rio Negro but in many of the smaller streams and lakes, some of which have the so-called white water. Interestingly, the *Symphysodon discus* that end up in the tropical fish importers' tanks in the United States and in Europe are always at least 3 inches in size. No explanation about why tiny *Symphysodon discus* have not been caught has ever been submitted.

Through these waterways or *igarapes* the discus collector will find an almost cathedral-like silence. It is easier to fish for discus here as the shoreline vegetation is lower and not as thick as in the upper Amazon, where the jungle encroaches and almost strangles the river banks.

By my standards the most interesting and rewarding areas for discus collecting are west and southwest of Manaus. Starting from Manacapuru, Amazonas, 40 miles west of Manaus, a collector can fruitfully branch out in almost any direction. Discus take on a new brilliance in almost all of these waters. I traveled from Manaus into the Lago Grande de Manacapuru, a lake region, to the village of Sao Luis. This is about 50 miles from Manacapuru. While fishing for discus in this area I found many blue and part blue discus, and in one particular area a fish was found that appeared to be a part blue/Heckel discus. This blue/Heckel discus area must have been fished commercially because a fair number of medium size (4 inches) discus appeared in Miami, Florida, at one time that looked exactly like the blue/Heckel cross I saw in the wild. I did not attempt to keep any of these blue/Heckel crosses, believing that they would be available in the exporters' tanks back in Manaus, but upon my return they were not available.

South-southwest of Manacapuru is the Purus River, probably the primary river region for colorful discus. A great number of the blue discus (*Symphysodon aequifasciata haraldi*) that are exported from Brazil originate in the many lakes and lagoons situated in the upper reaches of the Purus River. The fishermen in this area can get their catches of blue discus back to Manaus in less than two days.

Further west, approximately 350 miles from Manaus, *Symphysodon aequifasciata aequifasciata* (the Tefe green discus) can be found. Some of my Wattley turquoise discus stock has Tefe blood. The Tefe green discus inhabits most of the lagoons, small lakes, and streams near the very friendly town of Tefe. By American standards Tefe is certainly the cleanest and most comfortable of all the little towns along the Amazon between Manaus and Leticia, Colombia.

The Tefe discus appears to be a cross between the brown discus (*Symphysodon aequifasciata axelrodi*) and the more brilliantly colored Peruvian green discus. The muddy brown-green background coloring that most of the Tefe discus have is not apparent in the green discus from Colombia and Peru. I collected most of my green discus south of Lake Tefe, where the Tefe River meets the lake, although some were caught but a few hours from town. It was upon the advice of one Joao Benvindo, a local fisherman, that no time was spent on the Tefe River—malaria!

Continuing west-southwest the collector comes to the Jurua River. It is at this point, near Carauari, Amazonas, Brazil, that the actual collecting of discus becomes much more difficult. This is due to the fact that the shoreline vegetation of the stream is extremely dense and very hard to maneuver around.

Moving about in a small boat with a 25-horsepower motor on the rear allowed me to investigate many potential discus collecting areas from Carauari north to the tiny village of Curimata, a distance of about 25 miles. Many of the discus in this area were blue discus, probably *Symphysodon aequifasciata haraldi*, and many more were a mixture or a cross between blue, brown, and/or green discus. A very small number of the more brilliant blue discus, perhaps no more than two percent, had not only the bright blue horizontal striations throughout the entire body but also complete head maskings in the same brilliant blue coloring. It was a few of these Carauari blue discus with the exceptional head maskings that also helped me to develop my Wattley turquoise discus strain.

From Carauari the collector travels almost due west to a point where the borders of Peru, Colombia, and Brazil meet. Leticia, Colombia, is situated on the northern bank of the Amazon. It is here that any tropical fish collector fishing these waters makes his headquarters.

Just above its junction with the Amazon River on the Yavari River is the Brazilian outpost of Benjamin Constant. It is reported that there are blue discus in this area, although I did not fish there. Further north, well up into Colombia, I collected green discus (*Symphysodon aequifasciata aequifasciata*). This area near the town of Santa Clara, which is off

the Cotuhe River, can be reached by boat from the Putumayo River.

In my opinion the green discus in this region is the most exotic of all the Amazonian discus. Fished directly from its native waters, this discus generally has a basic background of an almost gold/mustard color. The turquoise-colored horizontal striations frequently run throughout the entire body, and the black border in the fins that surrounds the body is more pronounced than that of the Tefe green discus. In most cases the body above the lateral line, as well as a smaller area above the anal fin, will have the typical Peruvian green discus's red spots. In some cases these red spots appear throughout the entire body.

This Colombian green discus is very strong and easily adaptable to aquarium life. It can be successfully crossed with the blue discus (*Symphysodon aequifasciata haraldi*). By employing controlled breeding and the principles of genetics, some strikingly colorful offspring will be the result of several generations of breeding.

Green discus obtained from this area are taken from their point of origin to Leticia, Colombia, where they are air-freighted to European and American tropical fish importers. Fairly large numbers of these discus are generally available among Miami importers. This is only possible during the months of the year when the collecting areas are not inundated with flooding high waters.

CAPTIONS FOR PAGE 20
1. A turquoise male developed from the Wattley stock. This fish is defending and cleaning his spawn. Photo by Harold Beck.
2. A side view of the same fish as shown above. Photo by Harold Beck.

CAPTIONS FOR PAGE 21
1. A hybrid between *Symphysodon aequifasciata axelrodi*, the brown discus, and the blue discus, *Symphysodon aequifasciata haraldi*. Photo by Osvaldo Gonzalez.
2. This is a pair of hybrids. One of their parents was the famous Wattley powder blue discus, while the other parent was a brown discus, *Symphysodon aequifasciata axelrodi*. Photo by Dick Au and Wayland Lee.

Discus collecting trips in which I was involved differed from trips where the purpose was to obtain other species of tropical fishes. A typical general trip beginning in Manaus will carry the fishermen several hours upstream on the Rio Negro or 12 miles downstream to the junction of the muddy Amazon River. Along the way the gray-colored freshwater porpoise (probably *Inia geoffrensis*) can be seen swimming alongside the fishing boat, and on rare occasions a small group of huge pink-colored porpoises may also be seen.

Finally, the fishing area along the swampy banks of a small feeder stream will be reached. The boat will be tied up, and after jumping into the waist-deep water the fishermen will completely block off an area of about 20 feet along the weedy shoreline. All plants growing in this area will be cut and removed, thus making the already muddy, turbid water even more churned up. The net used to seal in the area is finely meshed and about 5 feet high, with 1-inch lead weights lining the bottom. The net will be slowly drawn toward the shoreline as soon as all the long grass is removed from inside the working area.

Up to this point not one fish will have been seen in the net area, but as it is gradually drawn up from the bottom and moved closer to the shore many fishes and river shrimp will be seen making frantic leaps to freedom. At this point the drawing of the large net will cease, and the head fisherman will dip into the very small, confined area and begin to net the fish. The catch will usually be quite bountiful.

Each dip of the hand net, which is about 18 inches in diameter, will bring up many tropical fishes. The fishermen will take an hour to capture and sort out the catch from each area. Each of these hour-long hauls will bring in at least 300 fishes. There will be many *Leporinus* and *Abramites,* as well as nondescript dwarf cichlids and plecostomus catfishes.

Interestingly, none of the fishermen have any fear of the supposedly dreaded piranha. They do show concern for the freshwater stingray though, and tell many accounts of fishermen who have been badly stung by the rays in the muddy waters. Likewise, *Hemicetopsis candiru*, a tiny 1-inch catfish, can cause problems as it is attracted to the odor of urine and is capable of swimming directly into human orifices. The fishermen protect themselves from the candiru by wearing tight-fitting underclothing.

The small river shrimp collected along with the fishes have a value. They are dried, ground up, and stored in glass jars as fish food to be fed mainly to cardinal tetras *Paracheirodon axelrodi* , the highest volume tropical fish exported from Manaus. Most of the cardinal tetras are collected several hundred miles northwest of Manaus near Tapurucuara in the small tributaries feeding into the Rio Negro.

On the return trip to Manaus the fishes are housed in large plastic pans approximately 9 inches deep by 18 inches long. Along the way are stations located on the main rivers that are manned by fishermen. These fishermen collect discus and *Corydoras* to sell to the collector in Manaus with whom they may have an agreement or to the first collecting boat that stops at their station.

No problem ever arises with the water in which the fishes are kept while returning to Manaus. This is because the water is changed frequently directly from the river. Once in town the collector will have facilities to pump clear river water directly into his tanks in the compound. From the time the discus or any other tropical fish is caught until it leaves the collector's compound it may have been transferred to any of the three waters of the Amazon (white, clear, or black). The differences in the chemistry of the three waters are so minimal that they will not affect the fishes.

On the Classification of Discus

It is not surprising that much confusion exists concerning the classification of discus. Adding to the confusion is much misrepresentation in aquarium literature concerning discus species, subspecies, color variations, collecting locations, and locations where no fish have been found. For the sake of brevity the Latin terminology as put forth by Dr. L. P. Schultz (*Tropical Fish Hobbyist*, 8(10), June, 1960) will be used. The reader will note that the general descriptions of the two species and the subspecies will be brief. This is because there is much color variation within the subspecies.

1. *Symphysodon discus* Heckel, 1840*
2. *Symphysodon aequifasciata* Pellegrin, 1903, composed of three subspecies:
   Symphysodon aequifasciata axelrodi Schultz, 1960 (brown discus)
   Symphysodon aequifasciata aequifasciata Pellegrin, 1903 (green discus)
   Symphysodon aequifasciata haraldi Schultz, 1960 (blue discus)

Symphysodon discus, the "Heckel discus," has also been referred to as the pompadour fish, blue Heckel discus, and red Heckel discus. This discus is truly unique, differing from the green, brown, and blue discus in several ways. The background body color can vary quite a bit, ranging from a brown-gray base to a honey-brown color. All true *Symphysodon discus* have the blue-colored striping throughout the entire body, although in most cases the blue color will also have a gray cast to it. It is not at all like the brilliant blue color of *Symphysodon aequifasciata haraldi*.

It would be difficult to select the most colorful or outstanding wild-caught *Symphysodon discus* from a group of 100, since they would probably all be practically identical in overall total appearance. It is very rare to find a *Symphysodon discus* superior in appearance to a group of others of this species.

As in all other discus, *Symphysodon discus* has nine black vertical bars. The fifth (middle) bar, however, is approximately twice the width of the other eight bars and normally is much darker than the others. This distinguishes the species immediately from all other discus.

The eye coloring of *Symphysodon discus* is basically the same as that of all other discus. In healthy fish that are free from stress and disease, eye color will vary from red to orange to yellow.

Symphysodon discus is a bit more retiring than the other species and subspecies of discus. It is not a shy fish, but it is not nearly as aggressive as other discus, especially at feeding time. If one were to keep six large *Symphysodon discus* in the same tank with six brown, blue, and green discus, the *Symphysodon discus* would herd or school together, whereas the other discus would not.

All full-sized adult discus, both *Symphysodon discus* and the subspecies of *Symphysodon aequifasciata*, whether taken from the wild or tank-raised, are basically the same size.

Symphysodon aequifasciata axelrodi is the discus most commonly available to the hobbyist. This is the "brown discus." The dominant background color of the fish is brown, but it can have overtones of gray, yellow, orange, or even red. Bright blue

CAPTIONS FOR PAGE 24
1. A Wattley royal blue discus, one of the first of the fancy discus to be derived from the Tefe strain.
2. Some of the initial breeding stock Wattley used were the green discus, *Symphysodon aequifasciata aequifasciata* (upper fish) and *Symphysodon aequifasciata haraldi*, the blue discus (lower fish).
3. The Bangkok red discus strain. This fast-growing strain is 4½ inches long in 6 months and breeds in 9 months, with broods of 150-200 fish all looking alike. Photo by Lo Wing Yat.

CAPTIONS FOR PAGE 25
1. Almost ready for breeding. This is a cross between *axelrodi* and *haraldi*. Photo by Harold Beck.
2. A Wattley turquoise showing the magnificent metallic-looking forehead.
3. *Symphysodon discus discus*, the discus Heckel, crossed with an *axelrodi*, the brown discus. Photo by Harold Beck.
4. A Wattley turquoise male fertilizing eggs as the *haraldi* female waits in the background. Photo by Harold Beck.
5. An 11-month-old *axelrodi* crossed with *haraldi*. Photo by Tom Wattley.
6. A turquoise male guarding his eggs. Photo by Harold Beck.

---

* *Symphysodon discus willischwartzi* Burgess, 1981, is possibly a cross of *Symphysodon discus* and *Symphysodon aequifasciata axelrodi*.

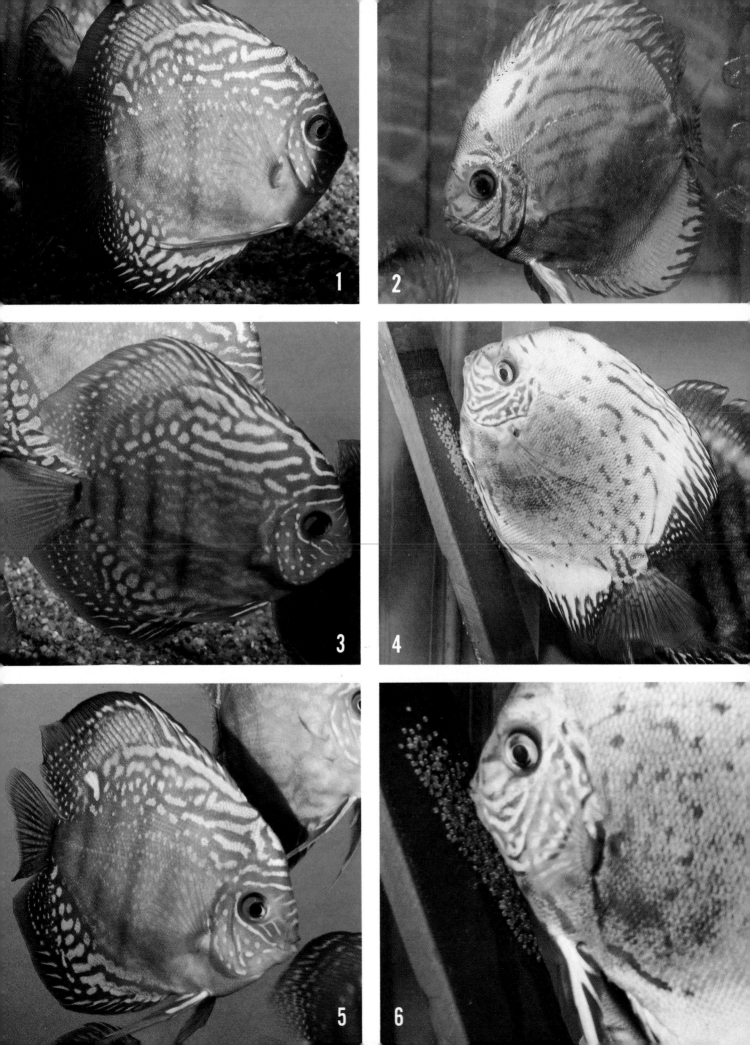

striations pass through the head and are generally found on the anal and dorsal fins of most individuals, but I have also seen many brown discus with virtually no blue coloring. Red coloring can appear on the anal and dorsal fins as well. There are nine black vertical bars present that are evident at one time or another. They are especially evident when the discus is in distress. A few years ago I developed a mutant strain of the turquoise discus that did not show the vertical bars at any time. Not much progress was made with the fish, and they ended up in the hands of several West German discus breeders. As with all other discus, the eye coloring of the brown discus can range from red to orange to yellow.

A large, healthy brown discus with delicate head and fin markings of brilliant blue is a beautiful fish. In the opinion of many, including myself, the brown discus can be as majestic-looking as any *Symphysodon discus,* blue discus, or green discus, although perhaps not as striking in color.

Symphysodon aequifasciata aequifasciata ("green discus") generally has a background color of muddy green or brown. In most cases any green horizontal stripes that appear on the fish will be quite brilliant in color. These green striations can appear throughout the entire body, but most often they appear on the head and on the dorsal and anal fins and do not develop in the center of the fish. Some of the green discus I have personally collected near Tefe have had the muddy green background coloring, while others (perhaps one percent) have had the brilliant green horizontal striping throughout the entire body.

These "Tefe green" discus may be a cross between the regular brown discus and the Peruvian green discus. The Putumayo River joins the Amazon River at the tiny Brazilian town of Santo Antonio do Ica, and it is from this area heading east to Tefe that the so-called Tefe green discus is found along with large numbers of brown discus. In this "highway of dispersal"—the area between the Putumayo River in Peru and the area of Tefe—the Tefe green discus has been found.

Other green discus that I collected in the Rio Cotuhe, north of the Putumayo River in Colombia and Peru, were much more beautiful, with some of them exhibiting the usual green striations. Most green discus, including the Tefe variety from Brazil and the Colombian and Peruvian green discus, have red spots throughout the body. Their anal and dorsal fins are bordered with a dark brown or black band, which makes these fish very attractive.

Symphysodon aequifasciata haraldi, the "blue discus," was named to honor the late Harald Schultz of Sao Paulo, Brazil, who did so much for the tropical fish industry for many years. Some credit should be given, though, to both Mr. Mike Tsalikis and Sr. Rafael Wandurraga of Leticia, Colombia. Mr. Tsalikis named the blue discus the "Tarzoo blue," with Tarzoo originating from the cable name of his company, Tarpon Springs Zoo.

It is the viewpoint of many that *Symphysodon aequifasciata haraldi* is nothing more than a very colorful brown discus with an abundance of blue horizontal striations. Both subspecies are collected in the same waters, although in some areas the blue discus can be found in greater quantities than the brown discus. An example of this is near the small village of Curimata, on the Jurua River.

In early 1960, the discus collecting area of Lake Manacapuru, Amazonas, Brazil, was discovered. This, along with the Purus River, is the home of a blue discus that has more brilliant coloring than the regular blue discus. This fish is nothing more than a blue discus with brighter color. In most cases the blue striations are found throughout the entire body, so the fish was called the "royal blue" discus by Brazilian tropical fish collectors in order to distinguish it from the regular blue discus. Needless to say, this "royal blue" fish commanded a higher price than the regular blue discus.

Unfortunately, today the name royal blue discus means very little, as fish constantly appear for sale as royal blue discus (and at royal blue discus prices) that are all too often nothing more than regular blue discus.

Equipment

Other color variations that have been given commercial names include the "Hong Kong blue" discus, which is a cross between the brown discus and the blue discus or the green discus. The "blue face" discus is nothing more than a brown discus that has been hormone-treated with methyl testosterone. The "candy-apple" discus is a discus raised in Thailand that has also been hormone-treated with methyl testosterone; this color variation is fed the bright orange eggs of the shrimp *Macrobrachium rosenbergii* which lends it the red/orange coloring in the facial area.

The "powder blue" discus is a beautiful royal blue discus with limited blue striations throughout the body and an overall powdery blue cast that covers the entire body. This blue coloring enhances the male discus only, for the female looks like a regular brown discus.

The "Wattley turquoise" discus that I developed has a brilliant turquoise blue coloring that encompasses the entire body. In most cases the female's coloring will be the same as the male's. Both sexes have bright red eyes. In fully developed adult Wattley turquoise discus the fin development is outstanding, with the dorsal fin extremely high.

When speaking of equipment, one naturally refers to the aquaria, heaters, nets, siphon hoses, plastic buckets, and all objects that when purchased wisely will make discus keeping easier and more enjoyable. It is entirely possible that the local water will be unsuitable for discus, in which case special (and usually costly) filtering equipment must be obtained. Most municipal water supplies are suitable for discus, however.

The question of which aquarium is best suited for discus is a topic open to much discussion. I keep my breeding pair of discus in square all-glass tanks of 21-gallon and 28-gallon capacity. Discus certainly do not show off their beauty and graceful movements in tanks as small as these, so if the hobbyist is not concerned with breeding the discus it would be best to try to obtain larger tanks. The standard 50-gallon size is perfect for four to six adult discus. The fish also adjust to their environment much better in a 50-gallon tank than in the narrower 55-gallon show tank that is longer but not as deep from front to back. Discus like the added depth that probably affords them a greater feeling of security.

A well-lighted fluorescent hood over the discus tank will show the fish to advantage. I do not use hoods over any of my tanks since I am constantly doing some sort of maintenance on the tanks and the hoods would be a hindrance to my work. The easiest type of tank cover to handle is made of plastic window screening with lightweight wood or styrofoam frames. Holes can easily be cut in the screening to allow for heaters and filter tubes.

Good quality airstones are needed occasionally, especially if a tank has to be treated with a medication that requires the cessation of all filtering during the time of medication. At that time one or more airstones, depending on the size of the tank, will be necessary. (A hint for the hobbyist: a 24-hour dip in a weak vinegar and water solution will open up a clogged airstone, thus allowing further use.)

Heaters and thermostats are of prime importance, so there is no excuse for purchasing an inexpensive or poorly made one. A discus breeder who is a good friend of mine

CAPTIONS FOR PAGE 28
1. Turquoise male with fry eating from his sides and with a Bangkok blue female in the background. Photo by Lo Wing Yat.
2. A pair of Wattley turquoise.
3. A Wattley turquoise with the spawning site (a plastic tube).
4. A pair of Wattley turquoise.
5. A hi-fin turquoise male with an *axelrodi* female. Photo by Osvaldo Gonzalez.
6. A hi-fin red turquoise with a deformed body. That didn't stop her from spawning on the flowerpot, however. Photo by Tom Wattley.

CAPTIONS FOR PAGE 29
1. Young breeding stock of Heckel discus and blue discus from Penang, Malaysia. Photo by Wong Chong Moh.
2. Young blue discus a bit stunted in size. Photo by Osvaldo Gonzalez.
3. Bangkok blue discus.
4. Wattley blue discus.
5. Wattley blue discus.
6. Wattley blue discus.

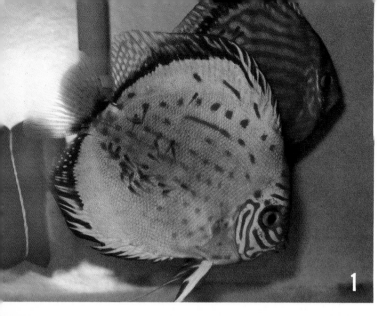

dates his heaters at the time of purchase and replaces them after 18 months of use. He has too many valuable discus to take any chances with a malfunctioning heater or thermostat.

An aquarium thermometer is another piece of equipment that should be of above-average quality. A photographer's darkroom thermometer is an excellent investment and will be completely reliable, unlike most of the tiny thermometers purchased in petshops. I can tell what the tank temperature is by simply extending an arm into the water, but there are occasions when an exact reading is necessary.

In reference to filtration, one must remember that regardless of the initial quality of the water the discus will alter it. Urine and fecal waste, as well as uneaten food, can cause a buildup of ammonia as well as a number of decay organisms (*i.e.,* harmful bacteria).

There are several approaches to filtration for the hobbyist. If one tends to be a bit lazy there is no better method than that of the biological sponge type. By following the manufacturer's instructions the hobbyist can determine what size or how many sponge filters will be needed. In a discus show tank one can employ the undergravel biological filter. The merits and demerits of undergravel biological filters have been known by tropical fish keepers for years, so it will not be necessary to discuss them here. Inside corner box filters or larger outside filters (generally hanging on the side of the aquarium) can be employed. When either of these two types is used the filter material is generally activated carbon (not charcoal) and Dacron. A medium grade silica sand can be used instead of the carbon with excellent results.

Generally speaking, there can be an increase in both the pH and the dissolved solids when new carbon is introduced into the filter. This is due to the alkaline salts that are used to activate the carbon. However, if new water is flushed through the carbon before applying it to the filter, the salts will not make a measurable difference to the aquarium water.

Most types of mechanical filters will in time also become biological filters housing beneficial *Nitrosomonas* bacteria. If biological filtration is desired in the discus tank the Dacron and/or sand should not be completely replaced at the time of cleaning. Leave behind about one-fourth of the old material, which will be holding enough of the beneficial bacteria to get things going again.

Some of the newer outside power filters produce a strong current in the aquarium, thus creating a condition that is alien to the discus, which come from very tranquil waters. It is for this reason that a much slower water flow is desired.

Peat moss (sphagnum) is also used by many discus and angelfish breeders, especially in Europe, to reduce the pH of the water. It has been conjectured that peat moss contains limited hormonal properties that enhance the breeding and the development of eggs of most South American soft-water tropical fishes, including the discus.

All types of filters have definite limitations, and it is up to the discus keeper to determine which filters will be the most efficient for his tanks. This determination will be based on the size of the tanks, the number of fish per tank, the frequency and the number of water changes to be made, and the type of feeding program that is to be used. For example, an overly zealous feeder using frozen beefheart or liver would require a more efficient filtration system than one feeding live foods, regardless of the fact that both parties would be feeding the same amounts of food and making the same sort of water changes.

Under certain circumstances no filtration is necessary. This "no filter" system is popular with the Asian discus breeders who have excellent water. Their discus are housed in bare tanks, only live food is fed, and as much as 90 percent of the water is changed daily. Therefore, they have no use for filters at all!

It might be said that to some extent the type of filtration used depends upon the quality of water being used. If the local water is a cornucopia of chemicals and is extremely hard and alkaline, the hobbyist will need proper filtration to make the water suitable for the discus. On the other hand, if the water is of a

Water Chemistry

good quality the method of filtration used will not be of paramount importance.

If mechanical filtration is to be used for the removal of excess food and waste material, it would be wise to know the quality of the filter and fully understand the functions and limitations of it. The reason for this is that many mechanical filters of inferior quality and design have appeared on the market during the past several years. The hobbyist might keep in mind that success with his discus will be in proportion to the quality of the equipment used.

After a discussion about filtration it seems most logical to follow with information about water chemistry. Some knowledge of discus biotopes is desirable, although it has been proved (especially in the United States) that duplication of those conditions is not necessary in order to successfully maintain and breed discus. The Amazonian waters where discus are found generally have pH readings of 5.5 to 6.8 and total dissolved solids of 10 ppm (parts per million) or less. This water could, therefore, be compared to rain water.

When the discus's water is referred to as being acidic, it is done in reference to the concentration of ionized hydrogen in the water. The hydrogen concentration is expressed as the pH of the water. The pH scale is logarithmic, so a rise or fall of one pH unit represents a tenfold change in the ionized hydrogen. The lower the pH the more acidic the water. Thus, a pH of 6.0 is ten times more acidic than a pH of 7.0 and a pH reading of 5.0 is 100 times more acidic than a pH of 7.0. Unpolluted rain water will have a slightly acidic reading of about 5.6 due to the carbon dioxide dissolved in it. Hence, the pH of the water measures only the amount of hydrogen ions present and nothing more. Impure, dirty water can have a pH of 6.0, but the cleanest, purest water can also have a pH of 6.0.

Therefore, the substance that makes the pH is what concerns the discus keeper. For example, a humic acid pH will be beneficial,

whereas a pH caused by sulphuric acid will be harmful to the discus. If the discus's water is maintained on the acidic side of the pH scale, this will automatically reduce the possibilities of a harmful bacterial buildup. In an aquarium the waste proteins such as those from excess food or decayed organic matter decay, resulting in the production of toxic ammonia, NH_3. The reduction of the pH to the acidic side of 7.0 plus the use of some sort of a biological filter will cause the conversion of NH_3 (toxic ammonia) to the nontoxic ammonium ion, NH_4+. Regular partial water changes should also be made to maintain this satisfactory condition. I have successfully kept *Symphysodon discus* in waters with a pH as low as 4.8 and as high as 7.5, but I would suggest a pH no higher than 7.5. There are many ways available to the aquarist of lowering the pH, so it should be a simple matter to maintain it within the range of 6.4 to 7.5.

To achieve an acid pH the choices that the aquarist has are phosphoric acid, hydrochloric acid, sodium dihydrogen phosphate (NaH_2PO_4), and sphagnum moss (peat). Naturally, if the local water is suitably acidic, whether it is treated city water, natural spring water, or well water, the above-mentioned chemicals and peat will not be needed by the aquarist.

CAPTIONS FOR PAGE 32
1. A 12-month-old brown discus, *Symphysodon aequifasciata axelrodi*. Note the wrinkles on the sides. This imperfection did not affect its spawning ability, nor was it passed on to the next generation. Photo by Tom Wattley.
2. Heiko Bleher, the largest discus wholesaler in Europe, with Dr. Eduard Schmidt-Focke in Bad Homburg, Germany. Photo by Christine Taras.
3. Brown discus, *S. a. axelrodi*, spawning. Photo by Osvaldo Gonzalez.
4. Brown discus guarding its eggs. Photo by Osvaldo Gonzalez.
5. Brown discus with fry eating from its sides. Photo by Osvaldo Gonzalez.
6. A brown discus with 36-hour-old eggs laid on the aquarium glass; a royal blue watches for the chance to eat the eggs! Photo by Osvaldo Gonzalez.
CAPTION FOR PAGE 33
Look closely at this magnificent fish produced by Dr. Eduard Schmidt-Focke. He calls it a green turquoise royally decorated with red spots in the middle of each scale that is not blue-green. This magnificent photo was taken by Heiko Bleher, who owns Aquarium Rio in Frankfurt, Germany. He sells the discus that Dr. Schmidt-Focke produces.

My water supply is from the city of Fort Lauderdale, Florida. It has a high pH reading of 8.0 to 8.5. For this reason the pH must be reduced. The preferred acids are sodium dihydrogen phosphate (NaH_2PO_4) and peat. Sodium dihydrogen phosphate is used in all my tanks except those housing confirmed breeding discus. The breeder tanks have peat to lower the pH to a desired 6.7. The reason peat is not used in all tanks is that most of my young fish are kept in conditions that would be considered a bit crowded. To compensate for the crowded condition in the tanks, large (40 to 50 percent) water changes are made daily with sodium thiosulfate ($Na_2S_2O_3$) added to neutralize the chlorine and sodium dihydrogen phosphate added directly to the tank with the fresh water. This is a very convenient and quick way to change large quantities of water.

The water in my breeding aquaria is changed several times a week, usually 15 percent each time. This city water is "conditioned" in a 250-gallon holding reservoir before it is added to each individual tank. Outside of the reservoir is an electric-powered canister-type German filter where the peat is housed and through which the water circulates at a rate of 500 gallons per hour. The weight of the peat moss being used is about one pound. It will take approximately three hours to lower the pH to a desired measurement of pH 6.7. Inasmuch as this water is not used every day, it has an opportunity to release the chlorine gas without the breeder having to add sodium thiosulfate.

Generally, the peat moss that is available to the aquarists in the United States comes from the state of Michigan or from eastern Canada. German peat is occasionally available. I have found that the best peat for my hatchery is that which comes from New Brunswick, Canada.

If the aquarist deems it necessary to lower the pH, he must do so with caution, especially if the water is soft. The soft water, having limited quantities of calcium and magnesium, offers no buffering effect against the acid being used. In such cases the pH can drop rapidly, causing an acid "burning" of the discus's fins and body.

There is a fair amount of variance among discus keepers concerning the frequency and amount of water changes. There are some successful breeders who change as little as 10 percent of the water every two weeks, and there are others who change as much as 75 percent of the water daily. I feel strongly that maximum growth of the discus can be obtained by making the larger changes, especially if one has been working with ideal discus water; additionally, the pollution level will be lower with the daily changes. In this case the huge water change would not be a great shock to the fish. It has been proved that as little as a 10 percent daily change is better than a 70 percent water change once a week. Even a 5 percent change per day is more advantageous than a 35 percent weekly change of water.

I have received numerous comments from people who have purchased a number of fish of approximately the same size at the same time, and within several months one or possibly two of these fish have greatly outgrown the others in the tank. Why? It is possible that this situation may be similar to that of the frog larvae. It is a known fact that frog larvae release a substance into the water that inhibits normal growth of other tadpoles in the same water. If the tad poles are unduly crowded the largest one will greatly surpass the others in growth. This largest tadpole produces something that will serve to inhibit the growth of the smaller ones. Possibly this is the reason that one young discus can outgrow all the others in a tank, in many cases to double the size of those remaining. This huge discrepancy in size exists even when there is sufficient food for all, with the same amount of food being available to all the fish. This extreme difference in size has never existed in my hatchery because of the larger-than-average water changes.

Is water hardness important? Yes, but in many cases it is not important enough for the breeder to be overly concerned with. It is known that discus do breed in the wild in water so lacking in calcium and other minerals that it is practically like pure rain water. Discus have also been successfully spawned in

Water Chemistry

extremely hard water, such as that in Los Angeles, California, where a beautiful strain of *Symphysodon aequifasciata aequifasciata* (green discus) was raised for many years in water with a total dissolved solids reading of 630 ppm.

The total dissolved solids scale actually measures the total dissolved solids, whereas the German DH (degree of hardness) scale measures only the total mineral content of the water. There has been much confusion about this. Hard water contains large quantities of metals such as calcium ions (Ca + +) and magnesium ions (Mg + +). These metals are not toxic to discus unless their concentration is extremely high. It is generally agreed that water of 1-50 ppm (total dissolved solids) is considered as being soft, and water from 50-100 ppm (total dissolved solids) is considered medium soft.

Most water available to the aquarist will no doubt be suitable for discus keeping, but if the hardness has to be decreased it can be done by mixing the hard water with distilled water or rain water or by running it over ionic resins. Distilled water is costly, a factor that must be considered, especially if one has to use large quantities. Rain water can be used to mix with the hard tap water to achieve the desired hardness, but it must be unpolluted rain water. Obviously, rain water collected in industrial areas heavy with noxious gases and pollution in the air would not be suitable. The removal of salts from the water can be accomplished (the result being water that is similar to rain water), but the equipment is costly and in nearly all cases it is not worth the time and expenditure invested.

There are some aquarists who use ultraviolet lights (germicidal lamps) to destroy harmful bacteria in their discus water. I have yet to see in all of my travels a truly successful discus program using ultraviolet lights. This also applies to the use of ozone, whereby O_2 (oxygen) is changed to O_3 (ozone). The use of this equipment is expensive, and if the aquarist adheres to a regular program of proper feeding and routine water changes they become unnecessary. A valid point to remember is that if the aquarium water will support the growth of green algae it will generally be suitable for discus. Brown or red algae generally denote poor water quality.

To conclude this chapter on water I have given a brief analysis of the city of Fort Lauderdale tap water that is used in my hatchery. As previously mentioned, with the exception of 24 to 36 hours of conditioning, the only manner in which this water is altered is in the lowering of the pH.

calcium	= 32 ppm
magnesium	= 1 ppm
sodium	= 1.5 ppm
iron	= 0.3 ppm
chloride	= 45 ppm
sulfate	= 25 ppm
pH	= 8.5-9

CAPTION FOR PAGE 36
This is an 11-month-old German turquoise discus raised by Dr. Eduard Schmidt-Focke in soft water with a very low carbonate hardness. Photo by Dr. Eduard Schmidt-Focke.

CAPTION FOR PAGE 37
A photograph of the holotype of the latest discus to be discovered by Dr. Herbert R. Axelrod. It was described by Dr. Warren Burgess as *Symphysodon discus willischwartzi*. This was the first "discus Heckel" type fish to be found south of the Amazon! Photo by Dr. Herbert R. Axelrod.

Jack Wattley's Handbook of Discus

The hobbyist is now ready to spend his yen, marks, dollars, or francs to purchase his discus.

They are not low in price, so the hobbyist will want to be in a position to make a wise decision. If the plans are to maintain the discus in a show tank, he may want to do some comparative shopping and then purchase several color varieties of the fish; but if the hobbyist plans to ultimately breed the fish, it is much better to try to obtain discus of the same variety or color and certainly of varied but similar sizes.

It is wise to ask the dealer for information about the number of fish originally in the dealer's tank and the length of time the discus have been in the shop. It is also important to find out how many of the fish have previously been sold and whether or not the remaining fish represent a fair cross-section as to size. The reason for this is that if the hobbyist selects only the largest fish from the dealer's tank it is possible that he may have taken all males since males are generally larger than females. On the other hand, if other discus enthusiasts have already purchased the largest fish the hobbyist may end up with all females.

It is redundant to say that the discus should have a good, natural color. Since the overall background of the many color variations will differ, the hobbyist is advised to immediately reject any discus that has a very dark brown or black background color. An unnaturally dark-colored discus is sick, and under stress all nine of the black vertical bars will be pronounced. However, if the fish is healthy the overall color will remain normal, not dark.

The eyes should be clear. The color of the iris should be red, orange, or even yellow, depending on the species or variety. For example, my Wattley turquoise discus generally have red irises.

The hobbyist need not worry about frayed or temporarily damaged fins. An increase in the tank temperature from 85° to 90° together with the addition of one-half teaspoon per gallon of noniodized rock salt will remedy this condition. Regardless of the condition of the fish, it is an

excellent idea for the first few days to raise the temperature in the tank to 90°. This temperature will increase the metabolism of the fish, and as a result they will be more inclined to eat and be more active.

In my opinion the most important thing to observe when buying discus is whether or not the fish is emaciated. This can best be accomplished by viewing the discus head-on. There should be absolutely no pinched-in look. The frontal area from the eyes to the top of the head and extending back to the beginning of the dorsal fin should conform gracefully to the rest of the body below the lateral line.

The discus should be taken home and initially acclimated on an empty stomach. This point is important because the move from the dealer's tank to the hobbyist's can create trauma in the discus, thus resulting in a digestive disturbance if the fish is moved on a full stomach. This digestive disturbance can also be compounded by the fact that the ammonia count, nitrate count, and bacterial count in the dealer's tank will probably differ greatly from the same counts in the hobbyist's tank.

Most wholesalers and retailers generally attempt to maintain their tank temperatures at 72° to 76° to conserve energy and because the majority of their livestock are most comfortable within this temperature range. Discus require a temperature of 82° to 86° and consequently suffer from the lower temperatures in the dealer's tanks. Therefore it is advisable to meet the discus's temperature requirements immediately upon transferring the fish to the new tank.

The pH will also have to be adjusted with care to match the pH in the water in which the discus have been kept until the time of their transfer to the hobbyist's tank. I am continually asked by buyers of my discus what pH I maintain in my tank (it's 6.8 to 7.2). Needless to say, hobbyists want this information in order to adjust their tank water in preparation for the arrival of their new discus. They are always told to carefully check the pH in the shipping bag when the fish arrive. A drastic pH drop

Purchasing

generally occurs during the time the fish have been in the plastic shipping bag, which may be several hours. This is perfectly normal, but the hobbyist should take that into account and adjust his tank water to that in the shipping bag at the time of the arrival of the discus. He can then raise the pH gradually to his desired reading over a period of several days.

A difference in total hardness between the dealer's tank and the aquarist's tank will not harm the discus. If the fish are purchased in the same town where they are going to be kept, the water hardness will probably be the same. However, discus can be moved from hard water to soft water or vice versa, and the change will have no effect on the fish.

Several other factors will affect the acclimation process, and paramount among these is lighting. Discus initially should not be exposed to any bright lighting. When lighting is intolerably bright, adaptation to the new environment can take an indefinite period of time. The lighting should be subdued.

Fishes of other species, such as scavenger types that can be nocturnal, can cause chaos for the discus by their nocturnal movements and feeding habits. Therefore, during the acclimation period the discus should not be kept with other species of fishes.

If distress occurs in the discus, the nine vertical bars will be clearly evident. Under normal circumstances, where the adjustment is not too great, acclimation may only take a few days and may be assumed to have occurred when the bars disappear.

Unless the newly-purchased discus are small, from 1 to 2 inches in size, it is probably a good idea to forego any feeding during the same day they are transferred to their new tank. It is wise to give them an opportunity to acclimate to their new surroundings before giving them an initial feeding. A cover over the tank might be in order as discus are jumpers, and the jumping tendency can easily occur during the period of adjustment.

After finally getting the new discus into the tank at home the hobbyist might wonder if his discus are truly what he thought he had purchased. If they are small fish of approximately 1 to 2½ inches in size they will not have any great degree of blue or green coloration unless they have been artificially color-treated. It is to the hobbyist's advantage to know his dealer well. With no true color as yet appearing on the discus, one has to rely on the integrity of the party who sells the fish. The dealer may tell the hobbyist in all honesty that the fish are of a certain color variety because he purchased them as such, whereas they could easily be nothing more than inexpensive brown discus. There is no tropical fish easier to "counterfeit" than a small discus!

Once the discus reaches the age of approximately six months one can fairly accurately ascertain what the ultimate color will be. If the hobbyist purchases his discus at this age he will naturally pay more for them, and in most cases the higher price will be worth it. If the hobbyist wants to be absolutely certain what color the fish will eventually be, he will have to purchase them as full-grown discus or at least as fish that are 12 to 15 months of age. At this stage the fish will have reached sexual maturity and should have their full color, although they will not have necessarily reached their maximum growth.

CAPTION FOR PAGE 40
This magnificent fish is only four months old! It was developed by Dr. Eduard Schmidt-Focke, and he calls it a hi-fin red turquoise. Photo by Heiko Bleher.
CAPTION FOR PAGE 41
During Dr. Schmidt-Focke's experiments with hi-fins, he developed a fish that was completely turquoise. This was the apex of his experiments. . .a high-finned, high-bodied fish with almost 100% turquoise coloration. No one to date has yet come close to this perfection of a turquoise. Wattley's turquoise is more metallic and a deeper color than Schmidt's.

One of the factors that will determine if one's discus will be maintained in satisfactory health and brought to their maximum growth is whether or not they are fed properly. There are many successful foods to be used, and over the years I have found that there is no secret food or formula that will ensure the total well-being of the fish.

For some time the partial diet of discus in Amazonia has been known. This consists of small freshwater river crustaceans that closely resemble the amphipod *Gammarus* and the larvae and pupae of aquatic insects. These aquatic forms of insects are similar to bloodworms.

Even though both of these foods are available to the average aquarist, it is not at all necessary for the hobbyist to include them in the discus's diet. Nevertheless, bloodworms can be purchased either live or frozen, whereas one must obtain live *Gammarus* from an aquatic supply house or from a grower of aquatic plants. *Gammarus* are the bane of aquatic plant growers as they feed on the plant leaves, so any grower should be happy to present the *Gammarus* as a gift.

On one discus-collecting occasion I dissected several discus I had caught in Tefe to see what food could be found in the stomachs. There was none. This may have been due to the fact that these discus were in an isolated, shallow stream during the dry season, and they may have been cut off from a regular food supply. I asked the local fishermen what the discus ate in those particular Tefe waters and was told *lima*, or algae. I felt certain that my fishermen friends were misinformed, however, for the green discus that were dissected were not emaciated in any way. It is quite possible that in the jungle streams discus eat when they can find food, but that there are many times when they go without food.

Although adult discus can go without food for great lengths of time, this situation, naturally, is not advocated for tank-raised discus. It does reinforce the fact that many hobbyists tend to overfeed their discus, although an overfeeding of live food would perhaps be a bit more permissible than one of rich, prepared foods.

It is known that protein is a major constituent of the discus's body and that a liberal and continuous supply is needed throughout its life. The natural diet of discus in the wild is rich in protein, but the minimum amount of protein needed to produce maximum growth in home aquaria has been poorly investigated. There are so many variables that affect optimum protein percentage in discus rations that it is difficult to recommend an appropriate level. Different environmental conditions would necessitate different protein levels. Certainly a pair of adult discus alone in a 10-gallon tank would require less protein (and food in general) than the same pair in a 100-gallon tank expending great quantities of energy while trying to defend a spawning site from other large discus in the same tank.

Protein quality is regulated by the amino acid composition. A ration with the highest protein quality is the one that supplies the necessary amino acids in optimal amounts needed for the discus's protein synthesis. Animal proteins in general have higher nutritive quality for discus than plant proteins do, and the hobbyist does have excellent choices of animal proteins for his discus: shrimp, liver, beefheart, and fish meal. Any or all of these high protein foods, combined with lesser amounts of carbohydrates and possibly fiber, constitute a suitable prepared diet for the discus. Carbohydrates are utilized by discus, but limited information is availabe about their digestibility and metabolism. Fiber is digested poorly by discus, and most of it may ultimately become a pollutant in the aquarium.

If one's discus feeding schedule includes several live foods, the addition of vitamins to the prepared food is probably not necessary. However, if the prepared mix is to constitute the only food, the added vitamins will then be necessary. The need for vitamins in the diet of discus is well documented, and they become more important when the discus are reared in an environment where natural live foods are lacking. Vitamin requirements are affected by

Food

the size of the fish, its age, environmental stresses in the tank, and water temperature. The complete effects of these variables are presently not known. I have found that the most acceptable manner of administering vitamins to the discus is by utilizing powdered health food vitamin supplements for humans. There are water-soluble vitamins for fishes available at petstores, but they are of minimal value.

These prepared powdered vitamins from health food stores also include minerals, which are also necessary to the discus's diet. However, as with the vitamins, the needs of discus for minerals are not yet understood. The aquarium water can probably meet some of these requirements. Calcium, for example, is often present in high concentrations in the water and may eliminate the need for a dietary source.

The powdered vitamin-mineral supplement I use is purchased in 8-ounce bottles and is mixed into the prepared food in the following ratio: 5 pounds of food to a weight of 0.2 ounces (5 grams) of powdered supplement. The following is an analysis of the vitamin and mineral content of the food. Each 5 grams contain:

B_1	25 mg
B_2	25 mg
B_6	25 mg
B_{12}	250 mcg
A	10,000 I.U.
C	150 mg
D	400 I.U.
E	25 I.U.
Niacinamide	100 mg
Inositol	150 mg
Choline	150 mg
Calcium pantothenate	50 mg
Calcium from bone meal	26 mg
Phosphorus (bone meal)	13.5 mg
Rutin	25 mg
Lysine	10 mg
Desiccated liver	50 mg
Biotin	20 mcg
Folic acid	0.1 mg
Iron gluconate	50 mg
Magnesium gluconate	7.2 mg
Manganese gluconate	6.1 mg
Potassium gluconate	10 mg
Copper gluconate	0.25 mg
Zinc	0.18 mg
Iodine	0.1 mg

The prepared mixed food that I advocate consists of:

3 parts uncooked fresh beefheart
½ part uncooked fresh beef liver
1 part uncooked fresh 3″ shrimp
¼ part cooked oatmeal
1/16 part raw wheat germ (partially for fiber).

The fat and fiber are carefully trimmed from both the heart and the liver and the chitinous shells of the shrimp are removed. All are mixed together with the oatmeal, and this mixture is put through a meat grinder once. The wheat germ and the vitamins are added after grinding. The prepared mix is then put into plastic bags and frozen.

I feel that this food is the most desirable improved mix that I have ever used in my hatchery. Over the years I have experimented with other mixes utilizing gelatin, cheese, cooked spinach, beef kidneys, and scallops and one can safely use any or all of these with beneficial results. One can also add a minimal portion of commercial tropical fish flake food to the mix without having to adhere to the same formula each time a new quantity is made.

CAPTION FOR PAGE 44
This native Amazonian can only think of discus as food. She was buying this fish in the Tefe fish market. Photo by Dr. Herbert R. Axelrod.

CAPTION FOR PAGE 45
A normal, healthy brown discus, *Symphysodon aequifasciata axelrodi*.

Other frozen foods that healthy discus accept are adult brine shrimp (*Artemia salina*) and bloodworms. The frozen *Artemia* must be of good color and consistency; brown, orange, or even greenish colors are acceptable, but never black. Frozen *Artemia* that are black in color will cause digestive disorders quickly, for having been defrosted and refrozen it is not at all suitable as a fish food. It is a good idea to obtain the largest size package possible, as the small packages begin to defrost too quickly once taken from the dealer's freezer.

The frozen bloodworms are a valuable food for discus. All cichlids can be brought into breeding condition when these worms are fed on a regular basis. In the live form they constitute the only food for commercially-bred adult discus in Hong Kong.

Glassworms (*Chaoborus*), mosquito larvae, and daphnia are infrequently available in the live form, but they are generally available in the frozen form. All of them can be fed as supplementary foods for the discus.

All of the above-mentioned foods (beefheart, worms, daphnia, and shrimp) are available as freeze-dried foods, although I have never developed a great deal of interest in or enthusiasm for them. To a great degree this is because the foods in freeze-dried form have never been tested in my hatchery.

Tests have been made in my hatchery to determine the discus's growth potential, using the following foods in equal amounts:

Tank A:	*Tank B:*
Imported flake food	Frozen adult brine shrimp
Tank C:	*Tank D:*
Live tubificid worms	Frozen beefheart mix.

Four 10-gallon test tanks were used, with ten discus in each tank. All of the discus were of the same age and size and originated from the same spawn. The water temperatures were equal, as the tanks were kept side by side. Three gallons of water were replaced daily in each tank. Three feedings were made daily, with an excess of food being given, thereby assuring that each discus would get its share.

Half an hour after each feeding all excess food was removed by siphoning and replacing one gallon of water. In as short a period as 14 days the discus had become significantly different in size, though exact differences were impossible to determine by using only visual measures. The fish in tanks C and D were of the same size, while the fish in tank B were one-fourth smaller and those in tank A were nearly one-half smaller than those in tanks C and D.

Much discussion and controversy center around the subject of live foods for discus. Are the enzymes found in live foods needed by the discus? Are the hormonal properties of live foods indispensable? These are questions that are frequently asked by hobbyists. I feel certain that there is a therapeutic value in live foods that prompts the hunting and catching of the prey by the discus. (A point to consider, though, regarding freeze-dried tubificid worms is, does the process of freeze-drying destroy the harmful bacteria that might have been in the live worms? One will remember that in laboratory work live, cultured bacteria can be maintained indefinitely in a freeze-dried state!)

There are live foods available that harbor no harmful pathogens for the discus, several of which can be successfully cultivated. An excellent food is brine shrimp (*Artemia*). Most of the brine shrimp originate in Australia, Canada, the western United States, and Brazil, and I found a very limited source at one time on the island of Andros in the Bahamas. The eggs (cysts) are readily available from any tropical fish shop.

After the eggs have hatched the tiny *Artemia* nauplii are transferred to a larger container with a higher salt density. The size of the container, needless to say, depends upon the quantity of shrimp that will be raised to maturity. The salt density must be significantly higher than in the hatching container, with a hydrometer reading of between 1.025 to 1.035 being satisfactory. The water used can be ordinary tap water, and the salt can be regular non-iodized rock salt or table salt (sodium chloride). It is not at all necessary to include any additional minerals, vitamins, or trace

Food

elements in the water. Gentle air from a fine airstone is as beneficial as sufficient daylight. I grow my *Artemia* in direct sunlight all year long, and I maintain the water depth of the container at no more than 10 inches. The summer temperature can reach as high as 90° to 95°. The shrimp thrive at this temperature, whereas at temperatures of approximately 50°F or lower metabolism decreases to the point where they cease to consume the food.

Artemia are fed powdered baker's yeast mixed with water, enough of the stock solution being added to slightly discolor the water. As the *Artemia* grow they will consume larger and larger quantities of the yeast, resulting in one's having to feed them approximately every other day. Any overfeeding will quickly result in water pollution, thus killing all the shrimp. Under optimum conditions the shrimp should reach maximum size (approximately ¼ inch to ¾ inch) in about 18 days.

Gammarus (freshwater amphipods) can be raised in small aquaria very easily. Starter cultures of *Gammarus* as well as those of microworms can be purchased from biological supply houses or aquarium mail-order companies. At maturity the *Gammarus* are a bit smaller than adult *Artemia*, with a fairly hard chitinous shell. They are an ideal daily food for discus. *Gammarus* prefer hard, alkaline water that is well-aged and an optimum temperature of 75° to 80° for maximum proliferation. A small sponge filter that will not trap the *Gammarus* is desirable. Well-washed spinach leaves and dark green lettuce have been recommended as part of their diet, although I have found the dry flake food based on the alga *Spirulina* to be an excellent food. In a 10-gallon tank a teaspoon of *Spirulina* flakes is sufficient food for approximately 50 full-sized *Gammarus*. Generally, a once-a-week feeding is adequate. With a minimum of care *Gammarus* are very prolific, although sufficient numbers must be maintained as future breeders.

Microworms (nematodes) are a superb supplementary food for small discus when fed in conjunction with live, newly hatched *Artemia*. There are many different ways in which the worms can be cultivated, and all are comparatively easy. The method described here is the one that I use to grow my microworms.

The starter culture is housed in a shallow glass or plastic container that has a tight-fitting lid. Small air holes must be made in the lid. The layer of culture medium must be thin (½ inch in depth), and it consists of five parts cooked oatmeal or uncooked cornmeal and one part baker's yeast. The microworm culture is added to this mixture. As the worms are livebearing they multiply rapidly, ultimately crowding the surface of the medium and the sides of the container.

At the first stage in the life of the culture, the medium is light-colored and gives off a pleasant, yeasty smell. At this stage the microworms are just beginning to pack the sides of the container, and they may be fed to the fish.

During the second stage the culture is slightly darker in color. Now the worms swarm up the sides of the container and possibly even onto the perforated lid.

At the third stage the culture medium becomes brown in color and the worms no longer climb the sides of the container. It is at this time that a new culture must be made. This is approximately four weeks from the time that the initial culture was started. The new microworm culture must be seeded with a very small bit of food (and worms) taken from the old culture.

CAPTION FOR PAGE 48
A tank-raised hybrid from brown discus stock, bred in Japan.
CAPTION FOR PAGE 49
This is the fish that Dr. Eduard Schmidt-Focke calls the "royal Turkis." "Turkis" in German is "turquoise" in English. Photo by Heiko Bleher.

Enchytraeid worms, more commonly known as whiteworms, are an excellent live food for all fishes, including discus. They are about 1 inch in length. Whiteworms have always been heavily fed to tropical fishes by European aquarists, but for some unexplained reason they are not held in high esteem in the United States. Over the years it has been written that daily feedings of whiteworms can cause fatty deposits on the internal organs of fishes, yet several of the most successful discus breeders I know feed whiteworms in large quantities in their daily feeding programs with no ill effects whatsoever to their discus. In such cases the adult discus breed in a normal manner and the younger discus grow beautifully. The whiteworms can be cultivated in close-fitting wooden boxes, plastic boxes, or tropical fish shipping boxes made of styrofoam. The boxes should be at least 12 inches by 12 inches by 4 inches deep. The container should be filled to a depth of 3 inches with clean potting soil. The culture should be kept moist, but not wet, at all times. The ideal temperature for maximum proliferation of the worm is 60°. A lid, or at least a piece of glass resting on the soil, is necessary, and the box or boxes should be kept in at least semidarkness.

In my opinion a food for the worms that is far superior to the usual oatmeal or bread so often recommended in books is *Spirulina* flakes. The flakes are sprinkled lightly on the surface of the culture, replenishing them as needed. These *Spirulina* flakes are enthusiastically consumed by the worms, and unless too great a quantity is fed, there is no danger of souring the black soil. The quality and quantity of the whiteworm culture will be greatly improved by replacing one-third of the soil approximately every 60 days.

Another superb live food worth cultivating for discus is earthworms. Earthworms can be raised in almost the same manner as whiteworms, the only differences in procedure being that of soil depth and the size of the container. For optimum results the container should be at least double the size of the whiteworm boxes, and the soil depth should be approximately 8 to 10 inches. Unlike the whiteworms, which can be fed whole to discus, the earthworms should be cut into small pieces for feeding. They can also be purchased at most bait and tackle shops by those not inclined to cultivate them.

With these discus foods at the hobbyist's disposal, what quantities should be fed to the discus, and how often? In my hatchery young discus (the fry) are fed live, newly hatched brine shrimp (*Artemia*) after having fed for a week on egg yolk mixture (which will be discussed in the section on spawning). Not all of the *Artemia* hatch at the same time, so for approximately the first eight hours of the hatch one can be assured of a satisfactory quantity of newly hatched shrimp. The discus fry will still be feeding from the egg yolk after this seven-day period, so naturally the initial feeding of *Artemia* will also include egg yolk. As soon as it is determined that all the young discus are consuming the shrimp, the yolk mix can be discontinued. The shrimp are fed to the discus a minimum of four times daily, making absolutely certain that there are fresh shrimp in the tank at all times. This point is important whether the fry initially are raised by the parents or artificially. In both instances there will have been a constant food supply during the daylight hours, and this condition must be continued.

A thorough cleaning of the tank bottom is made one hour after the last feeding, at which time all hatchery lights are turned off. Approximately one-fifth of the water is siphoned out to make this bottom cleaning, and it is replaced with fresh water. It is important not to mix unhatched *Artemia* eggs with the live shrimp as the discus young will attempt to eat them. The cysts or shells are not digestible, and disastrous bloating of the fry can result if they are eaten.

At this point microworms can be introduced to the discus fry. It is suggested that they be fed as a supplement and not as the main diet. Another excellent food supplement mentioned earlier is live or frozen daphnia. As the young discus grow to a size of approximately ½ inch,

Food

finely scraped frozen beefheart mix can be introduced. The heart must be scraped to a consistency of peanut butter and then washed through a fine net before feeding. Several weeks after the fry have accepted the frozen beefheart mix, one can begin to include chopped whiteworms in the diet. Flake food can be included in the feedings at this time either as a supplement or mixed together with the heart. Cultivated (not wild) mosquito larvae will be readily accepted by the young discus, and as the fish grow in size the pupal stages of mosquitoes will be most beneficial to the fish.

At this time four to five feedings per day should be attempted, but as the young discus reach the size of approximately 3 inches the feedings can be reduced to three per day. As the fish reach 4 inches in size the normal number of adult feedings (twice daily) can be made.

One of the two daily feedings for the adult discus should include the beefheart mix. It must be fed with care as there is no better culture medium for bacteria in warm water than an excess of liver or heart. This food when given to adults is naturally coarser than that fed to the young discus, but it still must be rinsed through a fine net to remove all liquids. The hobbyist will find that the adult discus will eat for about 15 minutes, and except for the first several minutes when they are filling up heavily with the food, the rest of the time will be spent picking up the remaining food particles from the bottom of the tank. If at the end of a 15-minute period there is still food on the aquarium bottom, it is an indication of over-feeding. Needless to say, this excess food should be siphoned out of the tank immediately.

The second daily feeding can include some of the many supplementary foods mentioned, such as frozen adult *Artemia*, live *Artemia*, whiteworms, and earthworms. This feeding must be made in time for the discus to finish eating before the hatchery lights are turned off for the night. Any uneaten food is then siphoned out of the tanks. If the siphoning of excess food is not accomplished at this time it will be partially spoiled by the following morning and the discus will probably begin to pick at it before it can be removed.

While on the subject of hatchery lights, it is worth mentioning that some discus breeders insist on giving their fish light 24 hours a day. This practice is totally unnecessary. Discus are in a completely restful state while in darkness, with a much lower level of metabolism. This is perfectly natural. Once the lights are turned off in my hatchery they are not turned on again until the following morning.

Over the years live tubificid worms have been fed from time to time in my hatchery. From any discus breeder's standpoint these worms are certainly a paradox. On the one hand they can cause untold troubles (diseases), while on the other hand there is probably no fish food that will bring an adult discus into breeding condition faster. The fullest growth potential of young discus can also be reached by feeding live tubificid worms. Is it worthwhile, then, to feed the worms to the discus? At this point I would have to say no. By eliminating them from the discus's diet and feeding a well-balanced beefheart mix along with other live foods, a successful feeding program can be achieved.

CAPTIONS FOR PAGE 52
1. A breeding pair of royal blue discus. Photo by Dick Au and Wayland Lee. This photo was taken in natural sunlight; one fish is shown too dark, the other too light.
2. Osvaldo Gonzalez, who took this photograph, says they are brown discus.

CAPTIONS FOR PAGE 53
1. A hi-fin turquoise male with a brown female. Photo by Osvaldo Gonzalez.
2. A Wattley turquoise male and a blue female. Photo by Osvaldo Gonzalez.

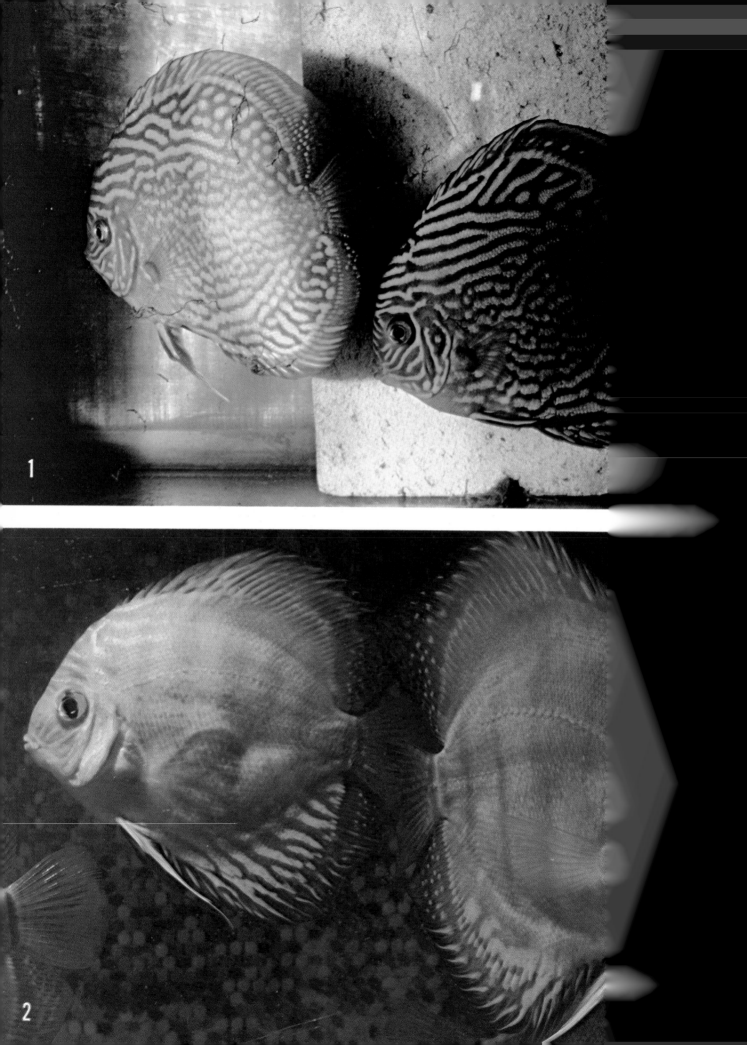

In their natural state tubificid worms thrive in polluted water, thereby playing host to many dangerous pathogens. The warm discus waters are conducive to bacterial blooms if the tubificid worms are fed in great amounts, so the discus keeper would be wise to eliminate them from the diet.

Some years ago I had access to a small worm-like insect larva that can be found in most stale or old bird seed. It would no doubt be difficult to find a cleaner, more desirable live food for discus. The yellow-colored worm is less than ½ inch in length and can be eaten easily by any adult discus. The worm is not available commercially and therefore would be of interest only to hobbyists who can maintain both discus and small bird cages.

Why won't my discus spawn? This is indeed a good question that I receive again and again from discus keepers who wonder why their discus will not spawn. The answer to the question may be very simple or very complicated. Is the water chemistry in balance? Are there a fertile male and a fertile female in the tank? Are they of age and in condition to spawn? What about tank lighting and positioning? Is the proper food being fed?

Discus must generally be about 12 months old before any spawning activity begins. My turquoise discus do not show much sexual activity before the age of 15 to 18 months. An excellent way to start proceedings is to put six or eight discus 10 to 12 months in age into a tank of at least 30 gallons. With this number of fish one is fairly assured of having at least one pair, although in many cases having both sexes in the tank will not be a guarantee of a "pairing off" with eventual spawning.

Is it possible to improve the chance of obtaining pairs of discus by distinguishing sexual differences in the fish? It is possible, but not too probable. Several years ago I had occasion to permit a self-professed discus authority to sex the fish in my hatchery. The

"authority" was allowed to study each tank, making notes of any physical and color differences of the fish. After approximately 30 minutes, the written results were handed to me. The "authority" was correct in 42% of the cases. Pure and simple guesswork could have achieved these results!

This self-professed authority also stated that males are more aggressive than females. I do not agree. A sexually mature female discus is in most cases more belligerent and dominant than the larger male. In a tank of six or eight mature discus, of which some are males, the sexually mature female will select her own mate by completely dominating him. At the time of the actual breeding it is she who will push or lead the male to the actual spawning site, and if there are other discus in the tank it is she, more so than the male, who will keep the other discus away during the preparation for the spawning.

Physical differences among discus are so varied that it is impossible to use them as a means to distinguish between the sexes. If one has three or four pairs of discus it is quite possible that the males will have more color than the females as well as differently shaped anal fins and lips. However, if one works with large quantities of breeding discus these physical variations may mean very little. It is generally agreed that in some cases the male discus will show more color than the female and may be somewhat larger in size. Conversely, I have many females that show more color and are larger than their male counterparts.

At the onset of the spawning act the reproductive tubes of the two fish will differ greatly, and it is at this time that the sexes can be easily distinguished. The female's tube (ovipositor) will be approximately two millimeters (1/12) inch in length and will have become greatly swollen and blunt, whereas the male's tube will be considerably shorter and a bit pointed. This greatly enlarged condition of the reproductive tubes will persist during the spawning act, and the tubes will gradually retract into the bodies of the fish after the spawning act has been completed.

After the proper water conditions and a good feeding program have been established and the discus are in excellent condition, the fancier may determine that the discus are old enough to spawn. What other factors are to be considered? I strongly believe that tank size, tank position, lighting, and even disturbances in the fish room are not of prime importance if the food and water conditions are in order. Naturally, if the discus are continually in a frightened state survival will become more important than reproduction and they will not breed.

My breeding tanks are 21 gallons; I find these to be more than adequate. It is a known fact that discus are territorially inclined. A breeding pair will generally claim a corner of the tank with their territory extending out from the corner approximately 12 inches. This area will be their domain, with the rest of the tank being almost totally ignored. Assuming that regular water changes are being made, it is not at all necessary to house one pair of breeders in a large tank. On the other hand, if the breeder is planning to remove the discus eggs from the tank and hatch them artificially, it is convenient to keep several pairs of breeders in a larger and longer tank, allowing enough space for each pair to have its own corner.

In reference to tank position, I have seen successful breeding pairs of discus kept in tanks on the floor (in Hong Kong), as well as in such high locations (in California) that a ladder had to be used to reach the tanks. From a convenience standpoint it is generally agreed that the best position for the tank is the one that can be easily serviced.

Many hobbyists have had successful discus spawnings with a bright aquarium reflector light shining directly down onto the eggs. I have seen the other extreme in Bangkok, Thailand, where breeders keep the discus rooms in virtually total darkness. But again, if the pairs are in excellent health they will certainly spawn in these or any other extreme environmental conditions. One point to remember, though. If the breeder plans to heat

the entire hatchery room rather than each individual tank, attempt to place all tanks neither too close to the floor nor too close to the ceiling. If the room is maintained at a temperature of 86°, the tanks close to the floor will probably show a temperature of 80° while tanks near the ceiling will probably be near 90° or more. In other words, all tanks should be placed at a certain height from the floor and a certain distance from the ceiling, thus assuring the fish of the right temperature.

Several years ago I partially remodeled my hatchery, and during this transition period the general atmosphere in the room was certainly chaotic. Apparently the fish were not affected by the carpentry work that created sudden vibrations or by doors that were abruptly opened and closed. Regardless of all the commotion, the fish continued to breed and eat in a normal manner during this five-day period.

In each of my bare all-glass tanks there is no equipment except for a small sponge-type filter and a piece of PVC plastic pipe on which the discus spawn. Many breeders employ inverted flowerpots in the tank or strips of either slate or stainless steel (such as those used by angelfish breeders) for the spawning medium. An aquarist can enhance his breeding tanks by placing plastic Amazon sword plants (*Echinodorus*) in the holes of the inverted flowerpots. In many instances the discus will choose to deposit their eggs on the leaves of the fake plants. However, since discus are substrate spawners they prefer to deposit their eggs on solid flat surfaces in either a diagonal or a

CAPTION FOR PAGE 57
This is one of Dr. Schmidt-Focke's brown pearl discus that he developed along with the red pearl discus. No one else has this strain at the time of this writing, but Dr. Schmidt says he will sell some soon. Photo by Heiko Bleher.

vertical direction. Wide-leaved living plants also make good spawning sites, and pieces of well-cured driftwood and tree roots are used by some discus breeders.

If the breeder plans to hatch the discus eggs artificially, the spawning medium should be small enough to fit into the hatching container. It is for this reason that flowerpots or PVC pipes are most advantageous. It is very frustrating, however, to have one or more spawning media strategically placed in the aquarium only to find that the discus have laid their eggs on a side of the aquarium, on a siphon tube, or even on a heater tube! I am of the opinion that the PVC pipes or stainless steel strips are the most suitable breeding sites for discus or angelfish. This is because they are not porous as are the flowerpots, thus lessening the chances that harmful pathogenic bacteria that could be housed in the pores of the pots might be present to damage the eggs.

Perhaps up to this point all is in order but the discus will refuse to spawn. If there are but two fish in the aquarium and they are a true, fertile pair, it may be necessary to introduce a third discus of the same size into the tank. A smaller discus will be totally ignored, while a much larger discus can become dominant regardless of sex and can disrupt the spawning process. Many times the addition of a third fish will arouse the dormant spawning desires of the pair, and almost immediately a lethargic pair of discus will be transformed into an excitable, sexually aroused pair. At this time they will begin to defend from the third fish the area in the aquarium where they will ultimately spawn. From this moment on all feedings should be made directly over the eventual spawning site. This will further arouse the pair to strongly defend their corner of the tank when they see the third fish venture into this area for food.

Without question the third fish must be removed from the tank if it is being totally intimidated and is suffering physical damage due to the constant harassment of the pair. Usually by this time, however, the pair will have had sufficient stimulus to proceed with their breeding preparations and the extra discus can be removed without interrupting spawning.

One can also add the third fish to the breeding tank but separated from the pair with a glass divider. The glass divider should be placed very close to the actual spawning site, with the pair on one side and the third discus on the other side. One added advantage to this approach is that if the discus pair do take care of their spawn the glass will act as a protector against the third discus. Tiny discus fry are not at all discriminating and will dash wildly to any adult discus in the tank and try to feed off its sides regardless of whether it is a parent fish or not.

Other methods to possibly induce breeding concern the changing of food and/or the altering of the water chemistry. Many times the hobbyist employs a monotonous feeding program, feeding perhaps nothing more than frozen brine shrimp or beefheart. The introduction of live adult brine shrimp and live earthworms will usually do wonders for the discus and will bring about the spawning of the fish.

Raising or lowering the pH can also prompt a pair of discus to spawn. Assuming that the normal pH of the discus water is 6.5 and a 25% change of tank water is made twice a week, the hobbyist can then discontinue major water changes for approximately two weeks, removing only excess food and fecal matter during this period. After the elapsed two-week period a larger water change of approximately one-third of the tank is made, but the incoming water is not adjusted to the normal 6.5 pH. Instead, the pH of the new water can enter the tank with a 7.0 to 7.4 reading. The one-third change of water and the increased pH can immediately act as a stimulus to the fish, especially since virtually no water had been changed during the two-week interim period.

This is not to say that either the addition of a third discus or the described one-third water change will guarantee spawning success, but in many instances it produces results. In my opinion the addition of the third fish brings the better results of the two alternate methods.

Regardless of the method used, the hobbyist

must keep in mind that to achieve total success in breeding discus several factors must be in order: the condition of the fish, the condition of the water, and the quality of the food. Many discus aquarists have isolated or temporary success in spawning their discus in spite of poor water quality or an inferior feeding program, but these are the ones who generally lose interest in their fish when the inevitable failures begin.

One can successfully breed discus even if one of the links in the chain of successful breeding is a bit weak, such as the feeding program being a little below par while all the other factors such as the water, the condition of the fish, the age of the fish, and so forth are in order. However, if the "little below par" feeding program is compounded by a below par water condition, then failure is inevitable.

Suppose at this point that all conditions are in order. What should the aquarist look for in the way of advance signs of breeding? First, one must be aware that nervous, jumpy discus make poor breeders, so it is hoped that the fish are well-established, that they come to the front glass in anticipation of food, and, unless unduly frightened, that they show no visible signs of nervousness.

The discus pair will choose their eventual spawning site, driving away any and all tankmates from the area. During the period of prespawning and adjustment, the pair will generally but not always partake in frequent little "dances." These movements usually consist of fluttering and quivering their bodies and fins as they "dance" around each other. In many cases the "dance" consists also of the tilting of their heads either upward or downward. These movements are accompanied by much tail lashing.

It is at this time that the caudal fins of both fish take on a black or dark gray hue. Without this very temporary dark coloration of the tail fin one can be virtually certain that the discus are not about to prepare for spawning. The normal head coloring of the fish also changes during this period, generally taking on a light brown or tan color. This light head coloring

also predominates whenever either of the pair is called upon to defend the spawning site from any predator. The predator can be another discus bent upon devouring the eggs or fry, or even the moving hand of the aquarist along the glass of the aquarium.

Some pairs of discus give advance notice of the impending egglaying, but others do not. Generally, though, the first prespawning act will be the cleaning of the surface on which the eggs are to be deposited. This act is a vigorous pecking and "mouthing" of the spawning area done by both the male and the female. This cleaning process has gone on at times in my tank so vigorously that the PVC pipes have been pushed from one side to another. This is accompanied by a horizontal head shaking by both fish. In most cases these prespawning movements take place one to two hours before the actual spawning. However, some discus pairs go through these movements sometimes for weeks with no actual spawning ever taking place. Conversely, some pairs give no indication of breeding until almost the moment before they actually begin the spawning act.

The actual spawning usually takes approximately one hour, during which time the aquarist must determine quickly if a true male and a true female are present. On rare occasions two females can spawn simultaneously on the same site, with the resulting eggs being naturally infertile. After viewing the ovipositor of the female and the

CAPTION FOR PAGE 60
This is a very poor photo of a red pearl discus developed by Dr. Eduard Schmidt-Focke. Photo by Heiko Bleher.

CAPTION FOR PAGE 61
This is the famous three-barred brown turquoise of Dr. Eduard Schmidt-Focke. Each scale is edged with brown. What a magnificent fish! Photo by Heiko Bleher.

genital papilla of the male, the aquarist will then be able to distinguish which fish is which. The aquarist should make a note of this for future identification.

It is poor judgment to attempt to view the total spawning act from very close because in many cases the breeding pair will associate the form of the aquarist with the distribution of food. If this is the case the spawning will be interrupted by the male or, more infrequently, the female (or both) moving to the front of the aquarium seeking food. Infertile eggs will be the result of this action if the female continues to lay eggs while the male shows more interest in feeding than in fertilizing the eggs.

After the determined female begins to lay her eggs, the male passes over the same site depositing his sperm over the first group of eggs. Approximately 15 eggs will be expelled from the female's ovipositor during each pass or "run."

The eggs are almost one millimeter (1/25 inch) in size, and their initial color can vary from a light amber red to a yellow-gray color. Some females deposit fertile eggs that are nearly translucent in color. Several years ago I had a female discus that laid bright red eggs, and nearly all of them were fertile. No, the fish was not a true red discus; it was nothing more than a *Symphysodon aequifasciata axelrodi* (brown discus) that I had bought in Thonburi, Thailand, to show to my family. The fish had been fed freshwater shrimp eggs (*Macrobrachium*), thus making it red in color. The color of the fish and of the subsequent eggs lasted for approximately three weeks, after which all red coloring gradually faded away.

In some cases the male discus will continually refuse to fertilize the eggs. Needless to say, if this condition persists one must attempt to obtain a more satisfactory mate for the female. In other cases the male discus will show more interest in eating the eggs after they have been laid by the female. However, even if the male or female is inclined to consume its eggs, this act usually does not take place until the eggs are approximately 18 hours old. About this time it is not unusual for a confirmed discus

egg-eater to swim directly to the spawning site and devour all the eggs within a time span of a minute or so.

This tendency of discus and of other cichlids to eat their own eggs has nothing to do with the fish being hungry at that particular moment. The fish may have been heavily fed with its favorite food and may still devour the eggs or fry minutes later. Undoubtedly an unsuitable water condition in the aquarium is a contributing factor to this egg-eating problem.

After the eggs have been laid the parents will faithfully guard them—at least for a while. While guarding the eggs, the parents will constantly fan them with their fins. Some discus breeders are of the opinion that the fanning is not to supply oxygen to the eggs, but it is rather a means of inhibiting foreign particles or fungus spores from settling on them.

If the hobbyist does not plan to hatch the eggs artificially, there is nothing to do at this point except to wait and observe. Observing entails watching the pair to make certain that they are totally compatible while they are guarding and fanning the eggs. Often one of the fish assumes a dominant role at this time, taking complete charge of the spawn and thus relegating the mate to a distant corner of the tank. If this inhibiting action becomes a bit violent it will be necessary to remove the weaker fish from the tank. The removal of the weaker fish should be of no great concern to the aquarist as the remaining discus guarding the eggs, whether it is the male or the female, will be quite capable of rearing the fry.

Naturally, having both discus parents raise the fry is more desirable, especially if there are a large number of young fish. A swarming, hungry mass of discus fry eating the body slime from the parents' sides and fins will take its toll from the feeding parents' energy.

At a water temperature of 86° the eggs should hatch within approximately 52 hours. At lower temperatures the eggs will take a longer time to hatch. During this 52-hour hatching period the parents spend their time fanning the eggs as well as picking off and

Spawning

eating any eggs that do not develop properly. In the process of eliminating any bad eggs a number of fertile eggs are inevitably eaten.

After the eggs have hatched, the fry can be seen wriggling in a little black mass attached to the spawning site. The hobbyist is overwhelmed with joy! An hour or two later he is beset by gloom—the fry have disappeared! Why? Perhaps they were eaten by the parents, but in many instances the young have simply been moved from the original site to another location. Many times this second location is a dark corner of the aquarium, but it can also be directly on the front glass. In any case, this moving about of the fry by the parents is seen as a protective measure against any predators.

After approximately 72 hours (again depending on the water temperature) the fry become free-swimming. At this point they will have used up the nourishment from their yolk sacs, and they will be actively seeking out the parents in order to begin feeding from their sides. Initially there are instances when the young discus swim aimlessly about the tank totally ignoring the parents. Is this because the parents do not have sufficient nutrient slime on their bodies for the fry? I believe that all adult discus maintain the body slime at all times whether or not they are raising young. On some breeding and nonbreeding adult discus the body slime is easily visible as a light gray color, whereas others have the secretion but it cannot be seen. On various occasions (generally to prove the point) I have placed young discus fry in tanks with placid nonbreeding adult discus and the fry have gone directly to the sides of the "foster parents" to eat with total success. At times, however, the fry were eventually eaten by the "foster parents" or the real parents. I have observed them until they were actually eaten and saw the fry hovering near the sides of the adult fish picking and eating the slime secretion.

An interesting point related to the above information concerns a pair of blue discus, *Symphysodon aequifasciata haraldi*, that I acquired from an aquarist in Miami. At the time of the acquisition there were seven-day-old fry eating from the parents' sides. In order to save time it was decided to take both the fry and the parents to my hatchery in Fort Lauderdale on the very day of the acquisition. The breeders were put into a plastic bag containing oxygen and the young discus were very carefully poured into a small, empty cardboard milk container. Upon reaching my hatchery and after the pair had been placed in their 21-gallon tank, the fry were slowly poured from the milk container directly into the tank. No problems arose. The young discus swam directly to the sides of their parents and almost immediately began to feed.

Frequently the adult pair will initially reject the tiny fry as they attempt to begin their first feeding. This temporary rejection can be observed by the aquarist. The parents will attempt to catch the fry and spit them back onto the aquarium glass or flowerpot. However, the young discus are persistent, and if all goes well they will eventually find their way back to the parents' sides seeking the nourishing slime. Once they are accepted by the adults, the situation settles down considerably and the fry begin their almost continuous feeding. In rare instances the young discus can be seen feeding from the sides of both adults simultaneously. In most cases, however, all the young will be found feeding from only one of the parents at a time.

CAPTION FOR PAGE 64
The #1 ichi-ban aquarium magazine in Japan is *The Fish Magazine*. It featured Wattley's turquoise discus on the cover of their January, 1981, issue. Photo compliments of Midori Shobo.

CAPTION FOR PAGE 65
This page from the Japanese ichi-ban *Fish Magazine* features the Wattley discus and even calls it that in English, too!! Photo compliments of Midori Shobo.

第17巻・第1号（通巻177号）昭和56年1月1日発行・毎月1回1日発行・昭和41年4月1日国鉄局特別扱承認雑誌第2332号・昭和42年2月13日第3種郵便物認可

フィッシュ マガジン

アクアリウム専門誌

FISH MAGAZINE

1981　1

人気沸騰
ワットレイターコイズがやって来た
バハマ諸島 アメリカの魚達
熱帯魚のふるさとアマゾン川魚類探索の旅(2)
折込コレクト版 熱帯魚大図鑑、海水魚大図鑑

ワットレイターコイズが当る
お年玉クイズ付!!

ワットレイ
ターコイズが
やって来た！！

This feeding action by the fry continues for approximately three minutes, after which time all the young discus are "transferred" from the "host" or feeding parent to the other parent. The transferring procedure can vary. In most cases, however, it consists of the adult with the young feeding from its sides swimming to the second parent. At the last possible moment it puts on a quick burst of speed as it glides past the other adult fish. This action actually brushes the fry off onto the second parent, who then becomes the feeding parent.

The tiny fry continue their quest for food without any interruption while the parent without the fry on its sides is given a moment of respite. After the two- to three-minute rest period the procedure of passing off the fry to the second fish will be repeated. This continues all day long. The postlarval yolk sac that gives initial nourishment to the fry can be seen as a tiny black dot in the stomach area of the fish. Once this "first food" is consumed and the fry begin to actively eat from the sides of the parents this black gut coloration will disappear and the gray color of the parental slime food will appear.

If the regular lighting is left on during the entire 24-hour period the young discus will continue to feed. Therefore, it is better to turn off all lights at the hour that the discus are accustomed to, or at least to turn off all regular lights, leaving but a very dim night light burning. If either method is used, the parent discus will probably "bed-down" the young fish by herding them into a secure corner of the tank until the following morning.

There are few times during the first few days of feeding when the parent discus allow the young to stray from their sides. For the first three or four days the fry will generally not venture more than an inch or two from either parent. By the fourth or fifth day the rapidly growing young discus will have doubled or even tripled in size. At this time they begin to venture away from their parents. These little "flights" of 5 to 6 inches away from the adults are very short-lived, usually not more than a few seconds duration, after which time the fry

resume their almost continuous feeding.

During the entire time that the young discus are dependent upon the parents for food they are totally responsive to any movements by the adults that might indicate danger. A sudden, violent twitching by either parent will send the tiny fry to their sides immediately, where they will remain motionless until the parents resume their normal swimming patterns. This shaking or twitching by the parent discus is basically the same type of protective action taken by many other South American cichlids.

Some discus pairs have a tendency to quarrel during the period that the fry are feeding from their sides. This is generally due to a reluctance by one adult fish to allow its mate to care for the fry. During the ensuing quarrel much bumping, fin nipping, and general cichlid-type fighting can take place. To the eyes of the hobbyist this scene looks like total chaos, as both parents are engaged in a jealous fight while the tiny fry are being swept wildly about the tank. Surprisingly, the young discus do survive the battle, and eventually things settle down. Needless to say, if the quarreling does persist it will be necessary to remove one of the parents. The remaining parent can adequately feed the young fish regardless of their number. After the fry are independently eating newly hatched brine shrimp and are removed to their own tank, the other parent can once again join its mate.

In most cases newly hatched brine shrimp can be introduced to the fry after the fourth day of feeding from the parents' sides. After gently washing the shrimp in fresh water they can be poured in or added with the use of a baster directly over the adult fish that is feeding the young. The fry generally ignore the presence of the shrimp—at least initially—but by the afternoon feeding or certainly by the following day they will eagerly seek out the baby *Artemia*. An adequate number of *Artemia* must be fed, i.e., enough to form a small cloud over and around the fry, because at this stage the fry will still not have developed the profound instinct to actively seek out a completely new and alien food. The orange-colored newly hatched brine shrimp can easily be seen in the stomachs of the fry. Preparations for moving the young can begin at this time. I generally leave the young discus with the parents for approximately one week, during which time the fry actively eat the body slime from the parents. After this seven-day period there is no great need for the fry to continue with the adults.

Water from the breeding tank is to be used initially for the transferred young discus. No harm will be done by netting the fry and transferring them directly to their new aquarium. The shock will be practically nonexistent since they will be going into the same water at the same temperature. In all probability the hobbyist will have a small fight on his hands as he witnesses the parent fish attack the "intruder", i.e., the net. I have seen many adult discus enter and attack a submerged net in their efforts to protect their brood.

The young discus can be housed very successfully in an all-glass tank of 5 gallons for the first month. A small sponge filter of any design or at least an airstone will be necessary. At this point daily water changes are important. If live, newly hatched brine shrimp are fed frequently throughout the day, the fry will have a tendency to perhaps overeat a bit. This eating to the point of looking a little bloated is not of any concern as long as the tank water is freshened with a daily change of about 20%. The new water will tend to keep the bowels of the small discus moving, thus helping to eliminate the possibility of any constipation problems.

Unless the hobbyist is working with extremely poor quality tap water, the 20% change of water can generally be added directly to the tank with no harmful effects. Naturally, if the chlorine content of the new water is excessively high it will be necessary to add a chlorine neutralizer. Needless to say, the new water entering the tank must not be cooler than the old. It can be at most 2° warmer than the tank water.

The procedure of a daily 20% water change can be successfully continued throughout the lives of the growing young discus. It does not have to be stopped once the fry have graduated to foods other than the young *Artemia*. After approximately ten days in the new tank the fry can be gradually introduced to finely chopped whiteworms, frozen and scraped beefheart, and crushed flake food. However, it is important to continue the daily feedings of newly hatched *Artemia*. The young discus will continue to eat the baby brine shrimp until they reach approximately 3 inches in size, as long as they are fed this food continuously. If the feedings are stopped for five or six days after the discus reach a size of approximately 1½ to 2 inches, they will not resume feeding on the baby brine shrimp, and the shrimp will probably be looked upon as nothing more than debris in the water.

As the young discus grow they must be moved into larger quarters. The advantage of initially housing them in a small all-glass aquarium is twofold. First, the smooth glass tank bottom can be cleaned in a more efficient manner than can a slate-bottomed tank, thereby controlling any waste buildup. Second, the discus fry not only feel more secure in the smaller tank, but the quantity of food can be more easily controlled. However, one negative point to remember regarding the smaller tank size is the greater possibility of overheating the water with a defective heater or thermostat. This actually applies to all small tanks housing tropical fishes.

CAPTION FOR PAGE 68
This hi-fin cobalt still has some growing to do, but Dr. Schmidt-focke considers it his finest strain because of the metallic sheen. Photo by Heiko Bleher.

CAPTION FOR PAGE 69
The strain for which Dr. Eduard Schmidt-Focke is famous is this light green strain that was at one time called the German turquoise, but after seeing the Wattley turquoise that name was dropped. Photo by Heiko Bleher.

From the time the young discus are taken from their parents until the time that they themselves (hopefully) pair off and spawn, there is no reason to differentiate concerning water quality between the adult discus and the young. In my hatchery all discus—adults, juveniles, and fry—are kept in water with the same pH and hardness. The water temperature does vary a bit, unfortunately, due to the fact that some tanks are located near the floor and others are placed considerably higher.

Undoubtedly the number one question concerning discus breeding is about the artificial raising of the fry away from the parents. If the discus fancier plans to raise the fry in this manner, there should be no live plants in the tank. This is because the receptacle where the eggs will be laid is to be placed in a small hatching container with some sort of a fungal and bacterial inhibitor that would surely kill the live plant or cause the leaves to disintegrate. The spawn might, unfortunately, be laid directly on the aquarium glass, but in nearly all cases it will be on the flowerpot, a piece of slate, or the PVC. As soon as the spawning act is completed the eggs can be removed to the hatching container. Some discus breeders leave the eggs with the breeders for about an hour in the belief that it takes that length of time to fertilize all the eggs with the free-floating sperm. In either case the eggs that have been fertilized by the male should eventually hatch in an approximately 52-hour time period. A 2-gallon glass hatching container is next employed. The water for the hatching container can be aged tap water that has been adjusted for temperature, pH, and hardness or it can be water taken directly from the breeding tank.

The medication I use to inhibit bacteria and/or fungal growth is methylene blue. To some degree the amount used is not overly important. Certainly 1 cc would be more than adequate. Moreover, acriflavine can also be employed in place of the methylene blue with satisfactory results. Both the methylene blue and the acriflavine act as light inhibitors during the incubation period, so it is not necessary to shield the hatching container.

Another antibacterial and antifungal agent that can be used successfully in hatching the discus eggs artificially is formalin (37% formaldehyde). Inasmuch as formalin is not a dye like acriflavine or methylene blue, it is better to completely shield the hatching container from as much light as possible if using formalin. Two drops per gallon of 100% formalin (a 37% solution of formaldehyde gas) in the hatching container is satisfactory.

Circulation and aeration near the eggs are necessary to ensure a good hatch. I achieve better results if the airstone is placed approximately 4 inches from the eggs. It is not at all necessary to use heavy aeration. In fact, a very mild stream of air will keep the water circulating around the eggs in a satisfactory manner. Aeration that is too strong tends to knock the eggs or the developing fry to the bottom of the container long before the fry would normally leave the spawning site.

After the eggs have hatched and the fry are in small, wriggling clumps on the bottom of the hatching container, they can be removed to their next aquatic home. This can be a glass kitchen baking dish, an enamel pan, or a shallow 4-inch aquarium. The best method of transferring the fry is with a glass baster. By the time the young discus have hatched in their original container, the dye from either the acriflavine or the methylene blue will have dissipated sufficiently to allow their removal with no problems.

The discus fry remain wriggling in little clumps on the bottom of their new home for approximately 72 hours at 86°. During this three-day period they receive nourishment from their own yolk sacs, and after a period of about two hours they all rise from the bottom.

Now is the time to introduce their initial food. Hard-boiled egg yolk will do, although better results will be brought about by using baker's egg yolk. The baker's yolk is comparable to freeze-dried yolk, so once a small quality of water has been added to it the consistency and properties become those of regular hard-boiled egg yolk.

Spawning

It will undoubtedly take some practice, but eventually the egg yolk mixed with water will take on the consistency of peanut butter. This will be accomplished by kneading the yolk with the water in the palm of the hand. The sticky egg food is then smeared around the water line of the aquarium using your finger. Logically, it is best to make a continuous linear feeding area since the fry do not actually seek out the egg food for the first several days; they just stay near the sides of the aquarium and continually dart from place to place. Therefore, it is important to have the egg food placed wherever they happen to "land."

With practice the hobbyist will be able to smear the egg food around the sides of the aquarium without any of it falling to the bottom. Very light aeration is desirable as long as the airstone emits a fine, misty flow of bubbles. If the egg application is such that it is a very thin, almost transparent film of food, the water will not have to be changed for approximately three to three and a half hours. On the other hand, if the egg food is smeared thickly it will be necessary to change the water after approximately two hours.

The water-changing procedure is simple, and the fry do not have to be removed to another aquarium. With a glass baster or medical syringe it will be necessary to remove as much of the old water as possible while making certain that none of the discus fry are sucked up in the process. During this procedure the egg food, if properly applied, will stay on the sides of the aquarium. Leaving only enough of the old water to cover the baby discus, the hobbyist should add new water very carefully until the egg food is again covered. By adhering to this procedure the discus fry will not have to be moved from one aquarium to another.

With several water changes being made throughout the day the film of egg food may become a bit too thin, and it may be necessary to replenish all or part of it toward the middle of the afternoon. Dispose of any of the egg food not used after each feeding. Nevertheless, after several days of applying the food the hobbyist will probably find through practice that the initial application of the day will last until the tiny fry are "put to bed" for the night.

All lights in my hatchery are turned off at approximately 11:00 p.m. It is at this time that the fry are moved to another small tank, using the syringe or the baster for the transfer. With a fair amount of dexterity the transfer of the fry can be made without putting into the new aquarium much of the old water that has been exposed to the egg food. The lights are turned off when the baby discus are in their new water, and they are left alone until the following morning. One important reason to maintain the discus fry in darkness during the night is that without light or food they will settle on the bottom and will not expend any energy darting about.

At this point it is probably important to state that where the term "new water" is mentioned it is to imply the same type of water as that used in the adult discus tank. If the fancier is using regular tap water for his adult discus with success, then the same type of water should be used for the artificially fed fry. If the hobbyist has to treat the new water for his adult fish by removing chlorine or altering the pH, the same steps must be taken for the fry's water.

CAPTION FOR PAGE 72
One of Dr. Eduard Schmidt-Focke's "new" strains. Schmidt breeds for intensity of color. . .the more color the better. This fish is less than 4 months old. Wouldn't it be a beauty at 14 months? Photo by Heiko Bleher.

By the end of the first day of egg feeding, the discus hobbyist should be able to detect whether or not the fry have successfully consumed any of the egg food. Their minute, black-colored yolk sacs should now begin to show a yellow-gray color. By the middle of the second day of feeding the stomach color should be yellow. If this is the case, the hobbyist should be on his way to success.

There are instances, unfortunately, when many or all of the spawn do not rise from the bottom on the first day that they are to eat away from the parents. There can be many contributing factors to such a situation. Is the water chemistry in order? What about the temperature? The ideal adult discus water temperature of 86°F will not allow the discus egg embryos or the young fry to develop properly. If the fry, for whatever reason, do not rise to eat at the time that they are supposed to, it is best to dispose of them and wait for the next spawning of the adults. If the adults are on a regular spawning cycle they should spawn again in about one week.

If all goes well (precise feedings and clean water changes) a noticeable growth will be seen by the third day. This normal growth pattern should parallel that of young discus that feed from the parents' sides. The growth rate of young discus, whether feeding naturally or artificially, is less than that of many other South American cichlids. Therefore, the hobbyist need not be discouraged if the fry do not look like baby oscars (*Astronotus ocellatus*) after the first several days of feedings. I also raise uarus (*Uaru amphiacanthoides*) in my discus hatchery, and after three or four days of feeding the uaru fry are almost twice the size of the young discus of the same age.

After the discus fry have been fed for six or seven days, most of them should be alive and well. Some will have died, which is to be expected, and some, being malformed, will have been discarded. It is at this time that live newly hatched brine shrimp can be introduced. It is impossible to state categorically that the fry can be started on the *Artemia* after four or five days. Generally, fry accepting baby brine shrimp at this age are from extremely large-sized parental stock. On the other hand, fry from small parents that are highly inbred will undoubtedly require six, seven, or even eight days of the egg yolk feedings.

In any case, the egg yolk is not to be suddenly discontinued when the initial *Artemia* feeding is begun. Some of the more advanced discus fry will immediately accept the baby brine shrimp, whereas others will still be totally dependent on the egg food. Therefore, the egg yolk should still be used until the sixth or seventh day. At this time, with brine shrimp also being eaten, the quantity of egg yolk used is greatly reduced.

Within an hour after feeding the newly hatched *Artemia*, the stomachs of the young discus will take on a bright orange color totally unlike the pale yellow color of the egg food. The egg yolk food can be discontinued when all the fry have orange-colored stomachs.

Feeding *Artemia* to the young discus is much easier than feeding the egg yolk. An overabundance of shrimp must be fed for the first several days. Again, this is because the young discus still have not developed to any great degree their instinct to seek out their food. The *Artemia* must be in front of them during the feeding hours to ensure their continuous feeding. After two or three days of this procedure the shrimp supply can be greatly reduced.

It is important to have brine shrimp available at all times for the discus fry to consume during the daylight hours. I feed the fry early each morning after making a one-third water change in the aquarium. Toward the middle of the day any excess dead shrimp are siphoned out, a small (one-fifth) water change is made, and fresh live shrimp are added. At approximately 11:00 p.m. the excess dead shrimp are again siphoned out as well as all of the live shrimp. Approximately one-third conditioned water is added, and all lights are turned off until the following morning.

If you adhere to this schedule of two daily feedings and water changes, the young discus will grow rapidly. At this time it will be necessary to make plans to move the fish to larger quarters where they will continue to grow in a normal manner. After several weeks of care it is not surprising to find a numnber of the young discus growing at a much faster rate than others from the same spawn. This is a good time to separate them according to size. By doing this the smaller fish should eventually reach about the same size of the larger ones.

Which method brings the best results to the discus keeper, leaving the spawn with the parents or attempting to raise the spawn artificially by feeding egg yolk? To answer this question satisfactorily the hobbyist must be aware of several points. First, there is always the risk that one or both of the parent fish will eat the eggs or the fry. Some pairs of discus are habitual egg-eaters. Needless to say, in cases such as these the artificial method would prevail. Does the discus keeper have the time to successfully raise the fry artificially? Some breeding discus show strong parental instincts, in which case it is perfectly safe to permit them to rear their fry. There is nothing more interesting and satisfying for the hobbyist than to observe a compatible pair of discus raising their own spawn in a natural manner.

Second, how many spawnings should the hobbyist expect from his pair or pairs? If the eggs are removed and hatched artificially the breeding discus will most probably spawn again is six or seven days. As long as they are on a regular spawning cycle the egg production will continue approximately every week. These spawning cycles generally last for 12 to 14 weeks, after which the fish enter into a rest period of approximately the same length of time as the spawning cycle.

During the rest period the female discus builds up her strength, and for this reason the feeding of good quality live food is recommended. The live food, along with frozen beefheart, will give the female discus the enzymes and proteins necessary for the buildup of more roe.

Many times during the rest period the male discus will show an intense desire to spawn. Totally frustrated by the female's inability to produce eggs and her total lack of interest in spawning, he may show his irritability by harming her by continual fin nipping, butting, and chasing. At feeding time the hobbyist will generally find the female cowering in a far corner of the tank, totally intimidated by the well-fed male.

If this condition persists for several days it will be necessary to remove the male discus or to place a tank divider between the two fish. I prefer the latter method, for in this way neither fish is removed from the aquarium and the divider can be removed from time to time to see if the male will continue his belligerent ways. Ultimately the female discus will again fill with roe, at which time the male can be moved back with her.

In the wild, discus probably spawn the year around. This is not to say that each pair breeds throughout the year, but rather that discus spawn during any given time of the year. It has been said before that the discus spawn only during the rainy or flooding season. The logic for this reasoning is that only at this time of the year is sufficient food found. It is certainly true that more insect larvae, aquatic worms, and tiny river shrimp are available during the rainy season. However, baby discus 1 inch long have been shipped out from Belem do Para, Brazil, at all times of the year, which disproves the conjecture of their spawning only during the flooding season.

CAPTION FOR PAGE 76
A magnificent three-year-old Chinese turquoise. Photo by Dick Au and Wayland Lee.

CAPTION FOR PAGE 77
This interesting albino discus never made a hit. Photo by Alfred Castro.

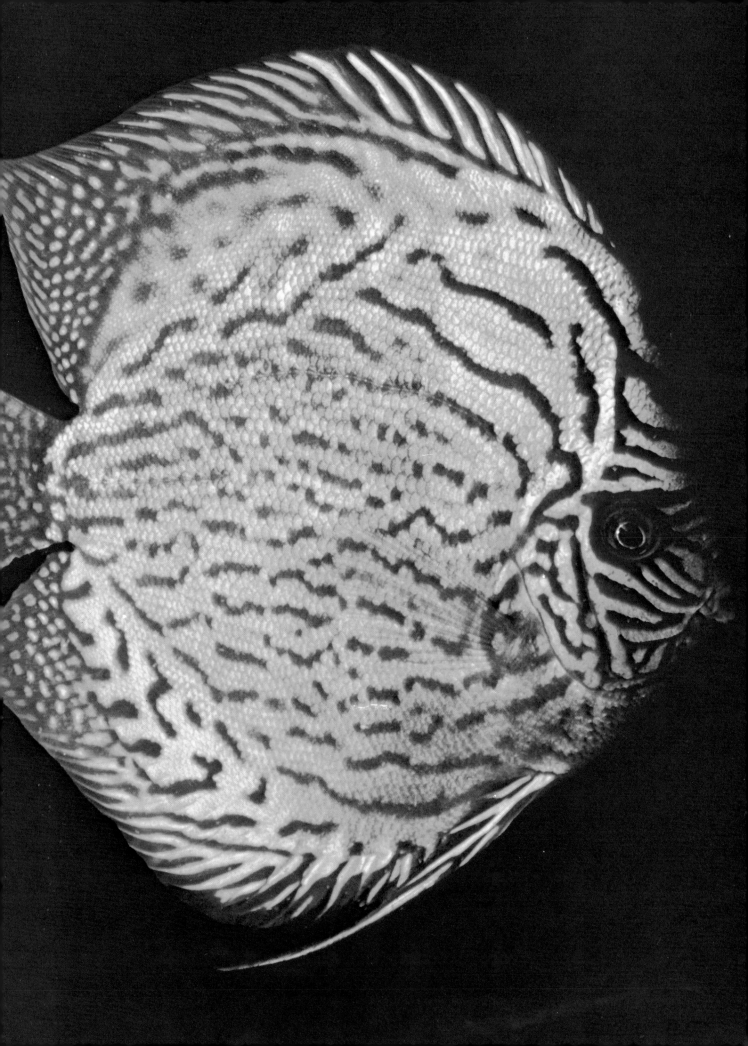

Because of the universal interest in discus, it is not surprising to encounter successful breeders in many countries of the world today. What is surprising is to discover that this success has been achieved under many varied and difficult conditions.

In both Jamaica and Trinidad, for example, beautiful discus are being successfully raised. Several of the Trinidad discus breeders have obtained breeding stock from me as well as from breeders in Europe, and they have maintained their success in spite of having to use water with a very high carbonate hardness. Although live food in the form of aquatic insect larvae is available these discus breeders rely almost exclusively on beefheart for their fish. Frozen adult brine shrimp are also fed, although mainly as a supplementary food.

European discus keeping centers around one country, West Germany. Contrary to popular opinion, not all German water is soft spring water. Some areas near the Taunus Mountains in central Germany do in fact have soft spring water with a very low carbonate hardness, while other areas, such as near Munich, have hard alkaline water. Why, then, have the Germans attained such a high measure of success with their discus? This is due to their attention to every important detail necessary for successful discus keeping. Their aquaria are kept scrupulously clean. To inhibit harmful bacterial growth many German aquarists employ ozonizers and/or ultraviolet lights, as well as large gravel biological filters. Prepared foods like those fed here in the U.S. are popular, with perhaps a bit more emphasis put on live foods.

The British have made rapid strides in discus keeping in spite of using water that is generally not the best for Amazonian tropicals. For this reason many of the British hobbyists have turned to deionizers to reduce the general and carbonate hardness of the water. With the possible exception of the Japanese, the British no doubt have the best available selection of discus to purchase. All species, color varieties, and sizes seem to be on hand at most times.

In Japan the selection of discus is very good, and the number of discus fanciers there grows daily. Recently, I gave a series of lectures about discus keeping in Nagoya and Tokyo, Japan, with a question-and-answer period following the lectures. Most of the questions directed to me (through a translator) indicated that the Japanese hobbyist is indeed quite advanced in the science of discus keeping.

Japanese discus keeping is similar in several ways to discus keeping in the U.S. The Japanese do not put too much emphasis on live food, instead using prepared beefheart as their principal discus food. As in the U.S., many Japanese discus fanciers prefer landscaped tanks with either live or plastic plants.

There is no commercial discus breeding presently being done in Japan, and most of the fish are imported from Bangkok, Thailand, with lesser numbers coming from Singapore, West Germany, and the U.S. Not too many years ago the Hong Kong discus breeders enjoyed a brisk business with the Japanese. Since the more colorful varieties of discus are currently popular in Japan, however, hobbyists have had no choice but to depend on the imports from Bangkok.

The largest discus breeding center in the world is Southeast Asia, including Hong Kong. Here the water quality is generally very good, and the discus are given excellent care by the Chinese breeders. Both Bangkok, Thailand, and Penang, Malaysia, have soft acid water, whereas the Hong Kong water has a pH of 7.5 but a general hardness of 1.0 to 2.0 and a carbonate hardness of 0.

Commercial discus breeders in Penang and in Bangkok take advantage of their excellent water to make huge daily water changes. I saw one Penang breeder change 50% of the water three times a day, once after each feeding. The same water conditions exist in Bangkok, where hatchery employees drain as much as 90% of the tank water, with the tanks being refilled by another worker immediately. This procedure is performed daily.

In the Bangkok tanks that house breeding pairs of discus, filtration is not employed, with the only piece of equipment being an airstone.

Discus Keeping Around the World

The discus spawn on small flowerpots. A few of the more ingenious discus keepers have devised a method to prevent egg-eating pairs from devouring their own spawns. Wire netting completely covering the flowerpot permits the pair to fan their eggs while not allowing them to eat them, thus ensuring a continuing interest in the eggs. The theory is that after the eggs hatch the parents will begin to exhibit their natural parental instincts in taking care of their newly hatched fry. Nevertheless, as many discus fanciers know, parent discus can just as quickly consume their own fry as they can the eggs.

At this point it is necessary to inform the reader that many of the discus (especially the young discus) exported from Bangkok are artificially color-treated. One of the finest foods to put rapid growth on small discus are the bright eggs of the native shrimp *Macrobrachium rosenbergi*. When fed these nutritious eggs, the young discus not only grow rapidly but also exhibit the orange-red coloring of the eggs throughout their bodies. If the Bangkok discus breeder wants to add an artificial iridescent blue coloring to his young discus, thus making them much easier to sell, he merely has to add 2 milligrams of methyl testosterone per gallon to the tank water. Within a few weeks he will have what is known as "blue face" discus, which are referred to among the Bangkok breeders as *Bum See Fa*. Both the "red" and "blue face" discus will begin to lose their artificial colors within three weeks upon the discontinuation of the *Macrobrachium* eggs and the testosterone.

Most of the discus that appear on Singapore price lists are fish that have been flown in from Penang and Bangkok, although I did find a few exceptionally successful Singapore hobbyists raising discus in their homes. These hobbyists had very few pairs of breeding discus, with the resulting young being sold to the local tropical fish enthusiasts.

One Singapore discus fancier gave me the following information about discus breeding in that country:

1. Discus pairs are kept in 40 gallon tanks.

2. Water changes of 50% are made daily, using tap water of 7.0 pH, but lowering the pH to 5.5 with liquid phosphoric acid.

3. No filtration is employed, with only a weak airstone per tank.

4. Food consists of live red tubificid worms and live bloodworms, after the worms have been soaked in a weak solution of a water-soluble vitamin B complex for approximately 30 minutes.

All of the discus I have seen in Singapore that had been raised by the above-mentioned breeder were very high quality *Symphysodon aequifasciata haraldi*, most being of true royal blue quality. This breeder was of the opinion that food is a more important factor than water in achieving success with discus.

Hong Kong discus breeding is done commercially on a large scale, with the hatcheries located in the New Territories, near the border of Mainland China. Across the border in Mainland China discus are now being raised commercially in Guangdong Province, near the city of Canton. All of these Canton discus are *Symphysodon aequifasciata axelrodi*, the brown discus, and are sold in Hong Kong for eventual export.

Most of the discus in Hong Kong are also of the brown variety, although a lesser number of so-called "Hong Kong blue" discus are being

CAPTION FOR PAGE 80
This Amazonian maiden from the Tefe area holds a weird looking fish. She found it in the fish market in Tefe, Brazil. Note that the forehead has *haraldi* blue stripes while the belly and flanks are marked like an *aequifasciata* green. Photo by Dr. Herbert R. Axelrod.

CAPTION FOR PAGE 81
The common brown discus, *Symphysodon aequifasciata axelrodi*. This specimen already shows the high-finned, high-bodied shape so desirable.

raised. This attractive fish has been available for a number of years and is no doubt a cross between *Symphysodon aequifasciata axelrodi* and *Symphysodon aequifasciata haraldi*. In most of these "Hong Kong blues" there are either blue striations or spots throughout most of the body, although this pattern is not nearly as intense as that of the true *Symphysodon aequifasciata haraldi*.

I sold a number of my Lake Tefe green discus, *Symphysodon aequifasciata aequifasciata*, to one of the largest commercial discus breeders in Hong Kong several years ago, but to date none of the offspring of these fish have appeared on the market. This Hong Kong breeder had 200 breeding pairs of brown discus, with each pair housed in a low 20-gallon tank. Each tank contained a small ceramic flower vase for the discus to spawn on. All Hong Kong discus, as well as those from Penang, Bangkok, and Singapore, are allowed to raise their own fry, as no artificial discus breeding is done in the Orient.

The Oriental discus breeders that I visited knew very little first-hand information about the feeding of prepared tropical fish foods such as frozen beefheart, flake food, or freeze-dried food; thus, they rely solely on live food. A very small daphnia is fed as the initial food when the fry are taken from their parents. This tiny daphnia is referred to as "dust daphnia." As the discus fry grow and are able to consume larger food they are fed live tubificid worms and/or chopped bloodworms.

The conditions for live food in Bangkok are different from those in Penang, Singapore, or Hong Kong. The Thai breeders maintain a continuous supply of live tubificid worms and mosquito larvae in their discus tanks throughout the day. The situation is quite different in Singapore, Hong Kong, and Malaysia, where heavy fines are levied against anyone found raising mosquito larvae! For that reason Singapore breeders feed their discus live tubifex worms and bloodworms, while in Malaysia live tubifex are the principal food.

In Hong Kong the major discus breeders originally fed their fish live red tubificid worms, but currently they are all of the opinion that live bloodworms are a cleaner and superior food. Today the more successful breeders feed their fish bloodworms exclusively. An interesting note is that live fully grown bloodworms can be purchased in every tropical fish shop in Hong Kong, whether it be an air-conditioned pet store or a tiny "sidewalk" tropical fish shop. Small portions of the worms are wrapped in newspaper and are sold to hobbyists throughout the course of the day for very little money. Another "sidewalk" fish food sold in Hong Kong that the local discus hobbyists are enthusiastic about is a 1-inch fresh water shrimp. This shrimp must be a comparatively new introduction to the Hong Kong tropical fish market, as I did not see them for sale there on my previous trips to the colony.

Before discussing discus diseases and medications it is necessary to redefine water hardness. Water hardness refers to the content of alkaline metals (such as calcium, sodium, and magnesium) in the form of salts of acids such as hydrochloric, carbonic and sulfuric. Depending on the quantity, these salts (carbonates, chlorides, sulfates) can affect the quality of the water that is available to the discus fancier. Too high a content of alkaline salts results in hard water and makes any dosage of medication difficult to determine. With the buffering effects of extremely hard water, the amount of most medications needed to effect a cure would be greater than in soft water with a low mineral content.

Very few, if any, of the commercially available tropical fish medications take this important point into account. The medications and the amounts that I suggest in this chapter can be used successfully in most waters that will maintain discus in a healthy condition. However, if the available water has a reading of over 700 ppm total dissolved solids, it might benefit the hobbyist to experiment somewhat

Diseases

with an additional amount of medication.

The pH of the discus water also plays an important role regarding the effectiveness of the medications. An example of this can be seen in the application of the sulfa drugs, which are not nearly as effective in acid water as they are in alkaline water.

An excellent way to determine if a discus is healthy is to compare the size of the eye in relation to the size of the body. On a healthy discus that has not been stunted in growth the eye should be approximately one-seventh the distance from the top of the black vertical bar that bisects the eye to the bottom of the bar at the bottom of the head. In instances where the eye is noticeably larger than one-seventh this distance, stunting of the discus is indicated. This could be the result of severe diseases or even an undesirable water condition such as a too high or too low pH or DH, infrequent water changes, or excessive ammonia or nitrites.

Modern tropical fish medicine centers around symptomatic treatment, which in itself will not alleviate the underlying cause(s). The cause of the disease is all too often purely speculative. Unfortunately, one tends to look only at the bacteria or other organism causing the disease. Since one would naturally prefer not to treat their fish for the same problem every six months or so for the rest of its life, it would be far more beneficial to know the cause of the disease, environmental or otherwise, so that the fish would never have to be treated again. It is known that bacteria often do not cause the initial infection, which may be the result of a lack of resistance in the fish.

Discus, as all other tropical fishes, are subject to external protozoan diseases, such as those caused by *Chilodonella*, *Ichthyopthirius*, *Costia*, and *Trichodina*. These diseases have been well documented in other aquarium literature and will not be discussed further. Regarding ich, however, there is absolutely no reason why any discus should ever be subjected to it if their water temperatures are maintained at 82° to 86°.

Stress takes on more importance with discus than with most other tropical fishes. It can cover a multitude of adverse circumstances, some of which can be difficult to recognize, such as low oxygen levels or chemical toxicity. Stressful conditions, such as ammonia and nitrite toxicity or fluctuations of pH or temperature, are easy to correct with the proper equipment, although a bit difficult to recognize.

Chemical toxicity, tank overcrowding, continuous abrupt vibrations, and excessive moving of the discus from tank to tank can all result in stress, thus becoming the forerunner of many bacterial diseases, as well as infestations by *Spironucleus* (previously classified as *Hexamita*). *Spironucleus* is a flagellate protozoan that many Central and South American cichlids harbor in their gastrointestinal tracts. This flagellate is a "debility" parasite that can rapidly cause problems with discus that have been subjected to stressful conditions. Transmission of the *Spironucleus* organism can be from other cichlids in the same tank with discus, with the discus being much more susceptible than the other cichlids.

Some of the more visible signs of infestation by *Spironucleus* can be the bloating of the lower gut area of the discus, stringy gray feces, signs of "hole in the head," or lack of appetite in the

CAPTIONS FOR PAGE 84
1. The Peruvian green discus, *Symphysodon aequifasciata aequifasciata*. Photo by Dick Au and Wayland Lee. These are probably bred fish and not wild ones.
2. These greenish blues are called "cobalts." They are produced by crossing *S. discus discus* with the blue discus, *S. a. haraldi*. The black in the tail and caudal peduncle has been inbred, and now there are "half-black" discus on the market. They are not popular.

CAPTIONS FOR PAGE 85
1. A *haraldi* blue female and a magnificent Wattley turquoise male with a lot of the metallic blue Wattley is striving for. Photo by Harold Beck.
2. Same fish as shown above except this features the *haraldi* blue female. Photo by Harold Beck.

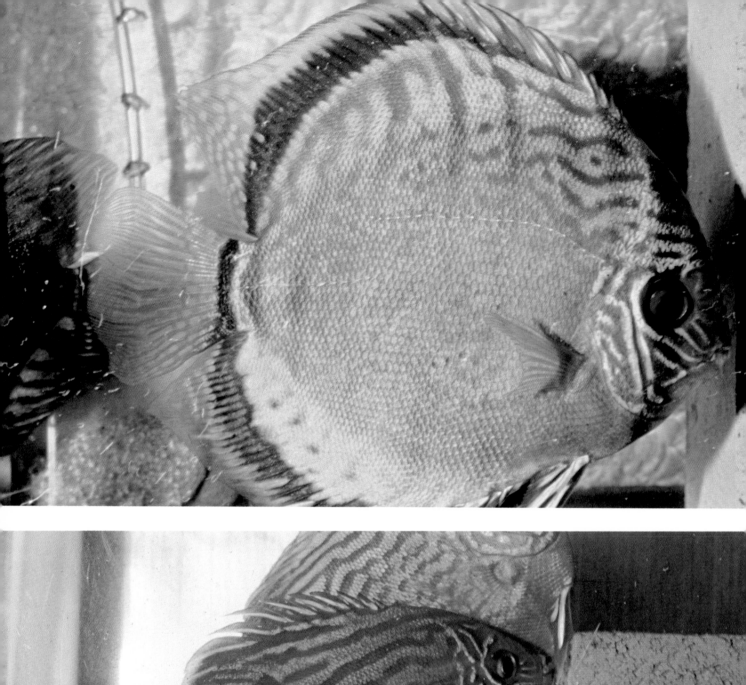

2

1

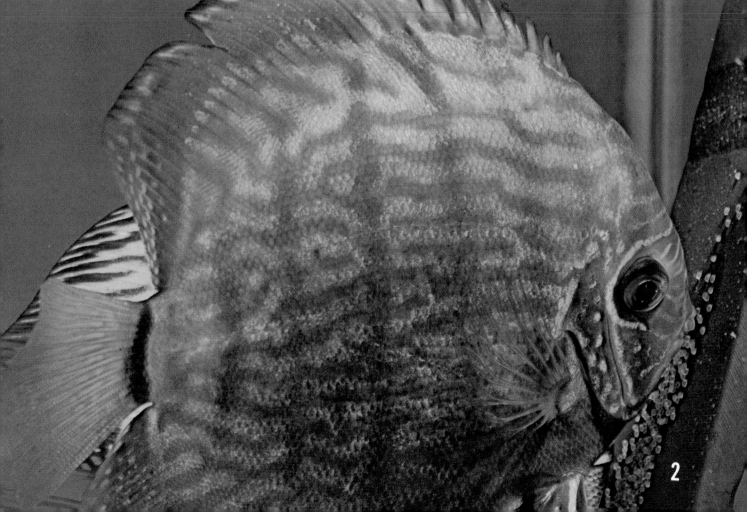

2

fish. Several medications that are easily obtainable will effect a quick and complete cure of such infestations. Metronidazole (flagyl) at a strength of 100 mg per 25 gallons of water for three days at 96° will produce a cure. During the three-day treatment period it is necessary to discontinue carbon filtration.

Another effective medication is ipronidazole hydrochloride (Ipropran) administered as follows: Mix 2.3 grams of Ipropran with 100 ml distilled water, then treat 10 gallons of tank water with 10 ml of the mixture. The initial treatment is to be followed by a second treatment 15 days later.

Certainly one of the most debilitating diseases that discus can encounter is infestation with *Capillaria*, a nematode worm that can be found internally in many cichlids. *Capillaria* is much more harmful to discus than *Spironucleus*. Effective medication is available, however, to combat this intestinal worm. The discus's refusal to eat, its "wasting away," and stringy white feces are generally the signs of infestation by *Capillaria*, although the white fecal matter can be the result of infestation by *Spironucleus* or of a digestive problem due to a poor feeding program. The medication of choice is di-N-butyl tin oxide at a strength of 1.0 ppm in the tank water for a period of three days.

Another remedy used by many discus hobbyists to treat *Capillaria* is Dylox (referred to in Europe as Masoten). Dylox, a white powder, decomposes rapidly at temperatures between 80° and 90° under alkaline conditions, and it should be used as soon as possible after it is dissolved. Use 0.5 ppm twice at 14- to 15-day intervals.

A *Capillaria* remedy employed by European discus fanciers is Concurat (tetramisole), a coarse white powder not readily available in the U.S. To 1 gallon of water add 10 grams of Concurat, after which a quantity of live tubifex worms is added. After a period of approximately 15 min utes, during which time the worms will have ingested a quantity of the Concurat, the worms are fed to the fish.

Two of the most common and bothersome parasites are the external flukes that usually attack the gills of the discus. Both *Dactylogyrus* (an egglayer) and *Gyrodactylus* (a livebearer) are easily transmitted directly by water and from fish to fish, with the parasite *Dactylogyrus* being the more debilitating of the two. I have found these two parasites to be more prevalent in European discus than in those in the U.S. with Oriental discus being virtually free from the flukes. These parasites are less than 1 millimeter in length and generally attach themselves to the gill lamellae of the fish.

Dactylogyris and *Gyrodactylus* can be found in limited quantities on healthy discus with virtually no damage occurring. The problem develops when, for whatever reason, the fish is weakened, at which time the *Dactylogyrus* or *Gyrodactylus* will almost certainly multiply in great numbers. At this point the flukes will affect the discus both by depletion of its oxygen and by the loss of the discus's ability to regulate the mineral salts and pH of its blood.

The rate of respiration of a healthy discus is more or less 60 times per minute, so it is quite simple to detect what could be either *Gyrodactylus* or *Dactylogyrus*. I have had complete success eradicating the gill flukes by using formalin, full-strength commercial grade, at three drops per gallon for eight hours. At the termination of this eight-hour period it is important to make a 40% to 50% water change. Needless to say, there should be no carbon filtration during treatment. If the flukes are the livebearing *Gyrodactylus*, one treatment will be sufficient, but if the unfortunate discus is harboring the egglaying *Dactylogyrus*, then a second treatment and possibly a third treatment will be necessary in order to kill the worms as they hatch.

There is much controversy as to during what intervals the second treatment should be made. The reason is that there are several known species of *Dactylogyrus* and their egglaying cycles differ. To be safe, I suggest a second treatment three days after the first treatment, followed by a third treatment three days after the second.

Another gill fluke remedy that is used mainly in Europe is Dylox (Masoten). The dosage, as for *Capillaria*, is 0.5 ppm. Medicate twice at three-day intervals with possibly a third treatment three days later if the fish show no distress. Under no circumstances increase the amount of the Dylox as it is stressful enough at the prescribed strength. When using Dylox it is normal for the discus to exhibit a slight temporary discoloration and loss of appetite.

There are instances where heavy respiration of the discus is the result of a bacterial gill disease. In such cases the medication preferred by many is nitrofurazone (Furacin). The dosage should be 10 ppm, and one treatment will usually be sufficient. Treating other bacterial diseases can be difficult if the hobbyist is unable to determine if the pathogen is gram-positive or gram-negative.

An excellent remedy for many gram-negative pathogens such as *Aeromonas* and *Pseudomonas* is gentamycin sulfate (Garamycin). This quite expensive drug is to be used daily for five days at a strength of 0.5 cc per gallon of aquarium water. Again, no carbon filtration should be done during treatment. It has been my experience that adding a pinch of powdered brewer's yeast to the tank water after treatment is sometimes helpful in restoring the beneficial bacterial flora in the intestinal tract of the fish.

Gram-positive bacteria can be attacked in many cases using erythromycin (Maracyn) with good results. The medication is readily available with instructions as to its use. Regarding any bacterial diseases affecting tropical fishes, it may be necessary for the hobbyist to try several different antibiotics, although not simultaneously, of course, in order to determine which will be effective. The bacteria involved may be resistant to many of the available drugs, but it is to be hoped that the bacteria will be microsensitive to others that are also available. In many cases it is of no use to raise the tank temperature to combat a bacterial problem because many gram-negative and gram-positive pathogens can tolerate the excessive heat much better than the discus can.

One may on rare occasions encounter a discus with a "bloat" condition, which is noticeable by a swelling in the lower gut region. Some gram-negative *Pseudomonas* bacteria can cause this swelling in discus. I have found that a rapidly developing bloat condition can be caused by a diatomaceous earth filter medium. Apparently, with the pressurized diatomaceous earth filter process the filter itself can pick up air and drive the oxygen to the upward limit of saturation. This causes an imbalance in the dissolved gases, which upsets the biological processes of the discus, manifesting itself as a bloat condition. Mechanically, the diatomaceous earth filters can also develop leaks on the suction side, thus pulling air from the atmosphere.

CAPTION FOR PAGE 88
Dr. Eduard Schmidt-Focke calls this his special strain. The fish is dark red on an almost velvet black body with bright horizontal lines shining like neon lights in fluorescent blue. . . sometimes in emerald green. That poetic language belongs to Heiko Bleher, who took this photo.

Jack Wattley's Handbook of Discus

by Dr. Herbert R. Axelrod

The world is full of dreamers. . . thank goodness. . . for progress in the world comes from these non-conformists. Where would we be without our Thomas Edisons, Alexander Graham Bells and the likes of Christopher Columbus and Jack Wattley?

Jack Wattley? Who is Jack Wattley? If you don't know who Jack Wattley is then you are certainly not well versed in the inner circles of the discus world. Discus? What's a discus?

If you don't know what a discus is, then you are certainly not well versed in the aquarium world.

The discus is a round, flat fish found in the Amazon River system of South America, mostly in Brazil. It has been the most expensive of the common aquarium fishes . . . the most sought after, and for many years the most difficult to breed. Most breeders were happy just to be able to breed these very sensitive fish, but one man had a dream that he not only wanted to breed them, but he wanted to study them genetically and to produce strains of differently colored discus which would be the envy of the world. His eye sought beauty that he could only imagine. Butterflies and orchids inspired the colors of his dream fishes . . . and though it took more than 20 years, his dreams came true.

Jack Wattley not only collected discus in South America, but he spawned them and inbred them for special colors which were then credited only to "dominant males."

Jack Wattley feeds his tanks personally. This gives him a chance to examine the fish more frequently. His son Tom assists him (in the photo on the facing page).

The Most Famous Fish Breeder

Wattley manipulated genes the way an artist manipulates a paint brush. His reward, aside from satisfaction of accomplishing a difficult life's ambition, was to become the most famous fish breeder in the world. Everybody knows about Jack Wattley if they know about discus.

HOW DOES JACK WATTLEY BREED DISCUS?

The reason for this postscript was a manuscript that Jack Wattley submitted to TFH for publication. It was a book about how he sought, caught and wrought the most beautiful discus in the world . . . the fish that is called **Wattley's Turquoise Discus.** When I read the manuscript I have to admit that a great deal of what Wattley wrote I did not agree with. As a matter of fact I was downright against publishing the book because of certain passages with which I violently disagreed . . . and I have a solid right to disagree with this book since I am the only person to have collected every species and subspecies of discus in their native habitat and range. With this background I *never* collected them in shallow ditches two feet deep, nor have I ever seen any natives throw the small discus

Wattley personally does the chores of looking for eggs (page 95) and inspecting for illness or disease (left). Wattley, net in hand, scoops out any ill fish, and treats it immediately.

CAPTION FOR PAGE 92
This is the first of the fancy discus. It is merely a brown discus, *Symphysodon aequifasciata axelrodi*, with intense red.

CAPTION FOR PAGE 93
Compare this normal brown discus, *axelrodi*, with the one on the facing page and you can understand why this was a "fancy" discus in the 1950's!

The Most Famous Fish Breeder

Wattley raises the baby discus in small trays. Each tray or pan is one spawn. These pans facilitate feeding and make changing the water much easier.

CAPTION FOR PAGE 96
Singapore blue discus with the fry feeding from their sides by eating the slime exuded by the parents. Photo by Dick Au and Wayland Lee.

CAPTION FOR PAGE 97
1. The eggs of Wattley's discus are artificially hatched in heavily medicated methylene blue hatching solution. The eggs are dyed blue in the process, but they hatch anyway. Wattley immerses the egg-bearing plastic tube in a glass tank (photos # 4 and # 8) until they hatch. Then he places the fry in a shallow pan (# 7) until they are large enough to eat live brine shrimp. They grow into magnificent turquoise-colored fish as shown in photos # 2, 3, 5 and 6. Photos by Dr. Herbert R. Axelrod.

The Most Famous Fish Breeder

Tom Wattley aerates the water in each pan with a syringe.

on the ground to die because they were too small to eat and not colorful enough to ship. Every discus I have ever seen collected was sold to a dealer who came around by boat and took everything they could get their hands on. They were all collected at night with a light, one by one.

So I gave the manuscript to others on the editorial staff of TFH. Neal Pronek, Jerry Walls and Dr. Warren Burgess all looked at me thinking, "Hey, this guy Axelrod is jealous or something" but they said "It's another point of view, we think it has a lot of

CAPTION FOR PAGES 100 and 101
These are the breeders that Wattley is currently using (December, 1984). Photos by Dr. Herbert R. Axelrod.

great material in it from the point of view of Wattley's personal experiences, and we recommend that it be published."

But how does Wattley breed discus? That's the real value of this book. First of all, he selects the fish from which he'd like to have breeding stock. These are highly colored fish, usually as turquoise-colored as possible, with the longest fins, too. Then he sets them up in an aquarium usually with 3-5 fish, hoping that nature will take its course and the fish will select their own mates. Experience has shown us that the first male and female to reach sexual ripeness will pair off and spawn. Then Wattley isolates the pair that show interest in each other and awaits the magic of reproduction.

He moves the pair to a breeding tank which is equipped only with a sponge filter and a piece of plastic pipe upon which he expects them to deposit their spawn. Once the spawn is deposited, he removes the pipe to a hatching aquarium. This is a small, all-glass battery jar, about a gallon in capacity. It is so darkly stained with methylene blue that you can hardly see the white plastic pipe with the spawn attached to it. The pipe works well since aeration is provided by pumping air into the center of the pipe thus affording gentle aeration to the eggs. Once the eggs hatch, the fry are removed to an enameled dish pan a few inches deep and about 12 inches in diameter. The fish are carefully observed hourly until they are free swimming and search for food. Normally at this time in their lives, the week old fish are searching for the bodies of their parents since the fry are parasitic on the body slime of their parents at this time. Wattley developed a scheme which insures a much higher survival rate than that allowing the parents to feed their fry.

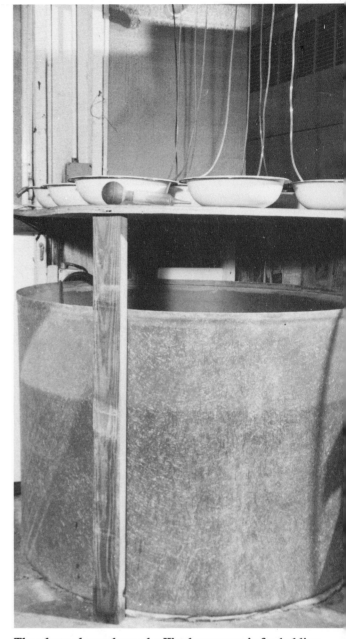

The photo above shows the Wattley reservoir for holding water as it ages. The photo on the facing page is the head of a 144-hour-old discus fry showing its well developed teeth. The cement glands are being absorbed, while the eyes and olfactory (smell) organs are becoming more developed. Photos by Dr. Harry Grier.

CAPTIONS FOR PAGES 104 and 105
The faces of Wattley's discus. Note the markings immediately above the upper lip. It is amazing how similar they are in many of Wattley's fish.

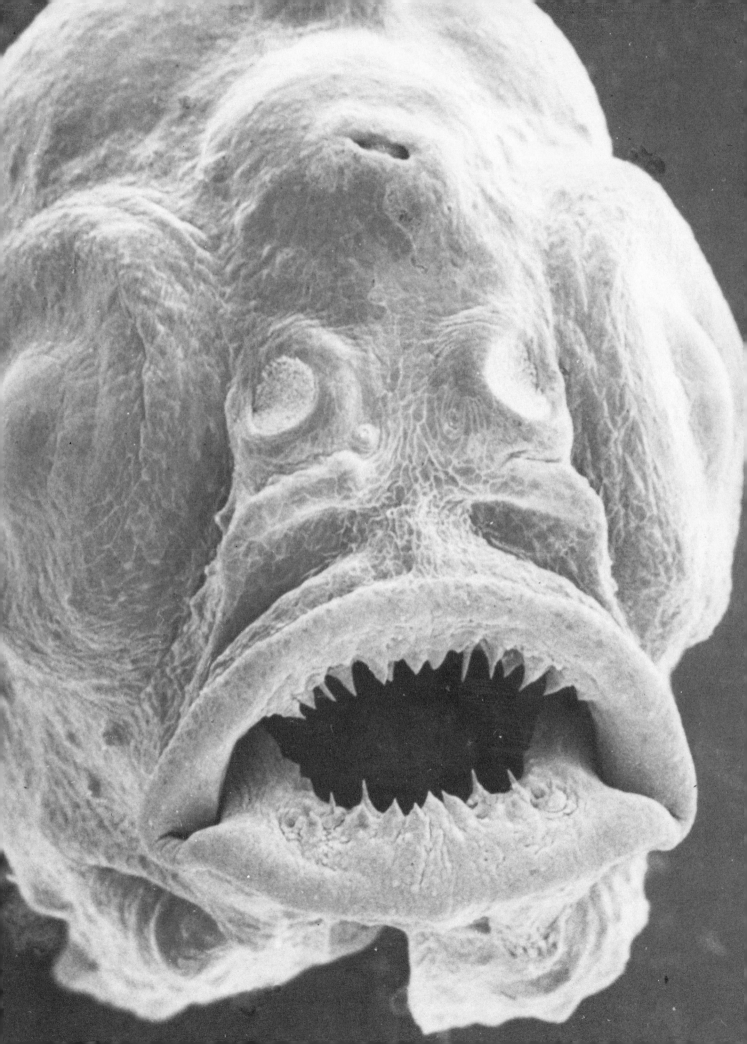

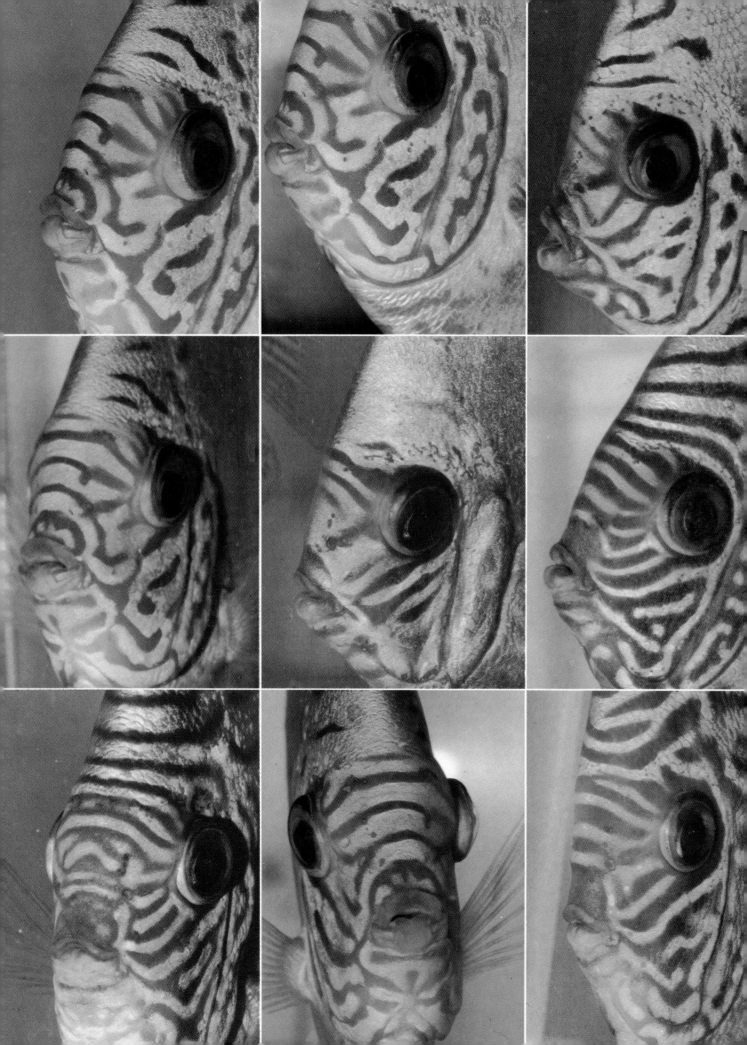

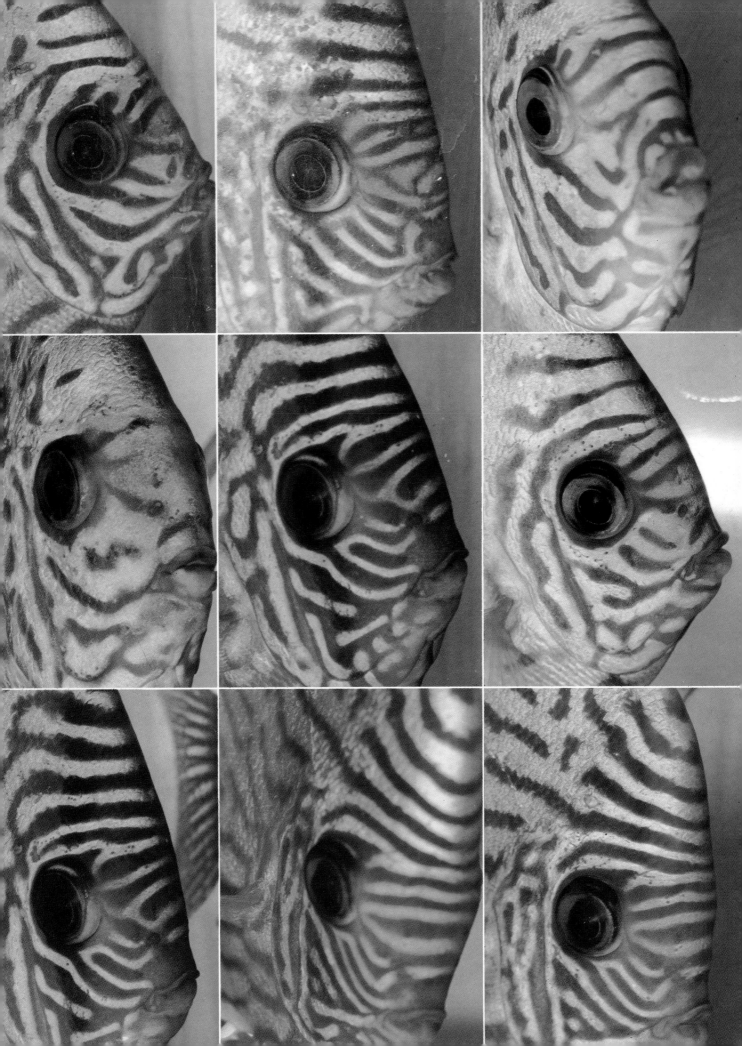

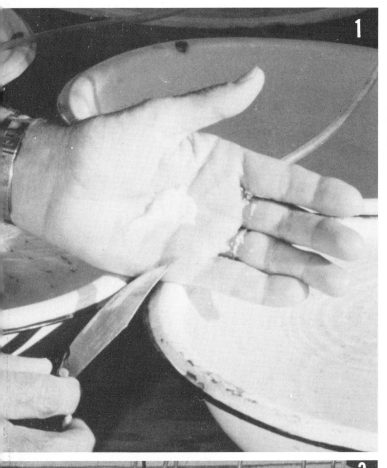

Wattley's preparation of his secret egg formula includes mixing it until it reaches the proper consistency (# 1). Then he uses his finger (# 2) to smear it along the meniscus of the water in the pan (# 3) so the fry can feed on it instead of on their parents' sides.

CAPTIONS FOR PAGES 108 and 109
This series of photos, top to bottom, left to right, shows newly free-swimming discus fry eating Wattley's egg yolk formula, then growing large enough to eat newly hatched brine shrimp, and finally becoming large enough to be fed Gordon's formula. On page 109 the closeups show the Wattley egg yolk formula being attacked by the hungry discus fry.

The Most Famous Fish Breeder

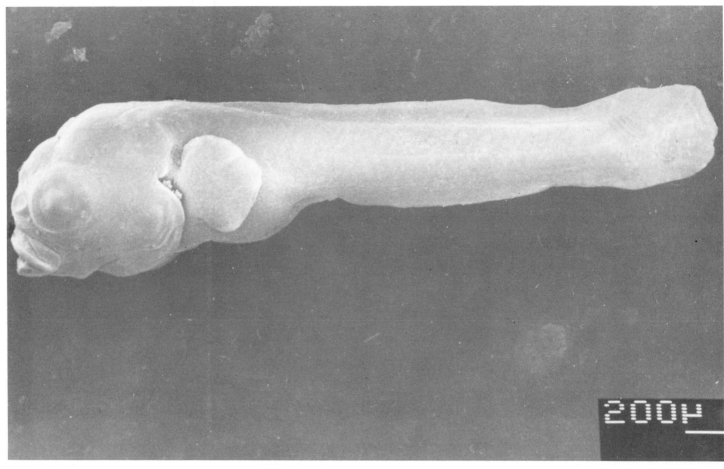

200µ

This fry is the same one as shown on page 103, being six days old with teeth sharp enough to gouge chunks of slime from the body of its parents. Photo by Dr. Harry Grier.

WATTLEY'S SECRET FORMULA

Wattley has developed a formula fish food which is composed mostly of egg yolk. He makes this formula into a paste and he smears it with his finger just below the edge of the water in the enamel soup bowl so the baby discus can feed from it as though it were the slime on their parents' sides. This really works well and as far as I know it is the ONLY method by which eggs can be taken away from discus breeders and hatched artificially. Naturally this egg formula fouls the water as the fish have to be fed continuously during their first few days of free-swimming life. Thus theirs is a lot of work . . . day and night . . . in changing the fish fry from one bowl to another.

After about a week of this feeding, Wattley uses newly hatched brine shrimp nauplii to supplement the diet. Once the larger fry begin eating the nauplii his task is lightened. He separates out the larger fry and feeds them brine shrimp while the smaller fry stay on the egg diet until they are large enough to ingest the tiny newly hatched brine shrimp. The fry are kept in the bowls for a few weeks, then transferred to tanks where they are fed a growing formula of brine shrimp and Gordon's formula. (Gordon's formula is a liver-based fish food in paste form which was developed by my teacher, Professor Myron Gordon. This formula can be found in most of the books I have written for beginning aquarists). In a month the fry are about the size of a quarter, DM or 10p piece and can be sold.

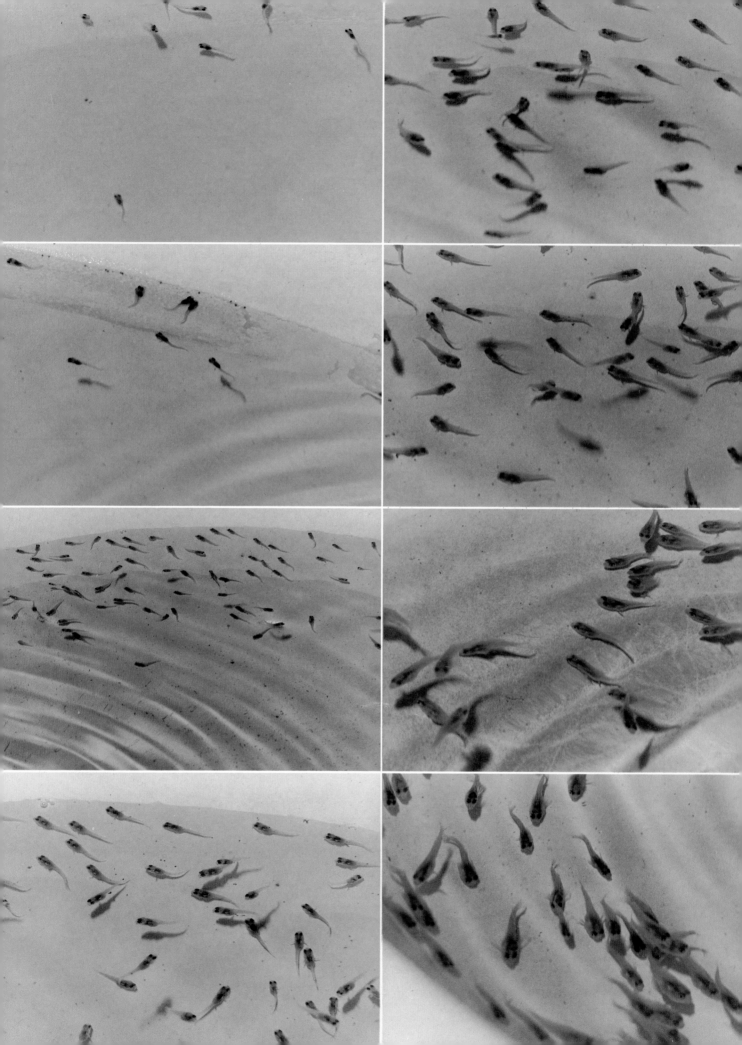

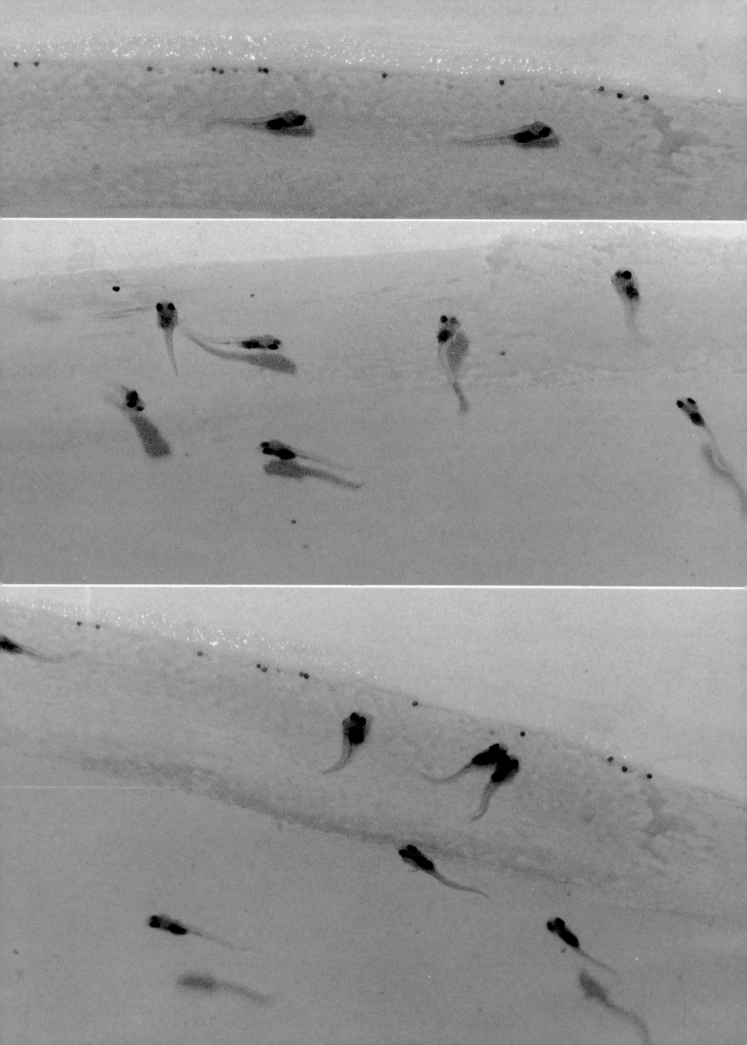

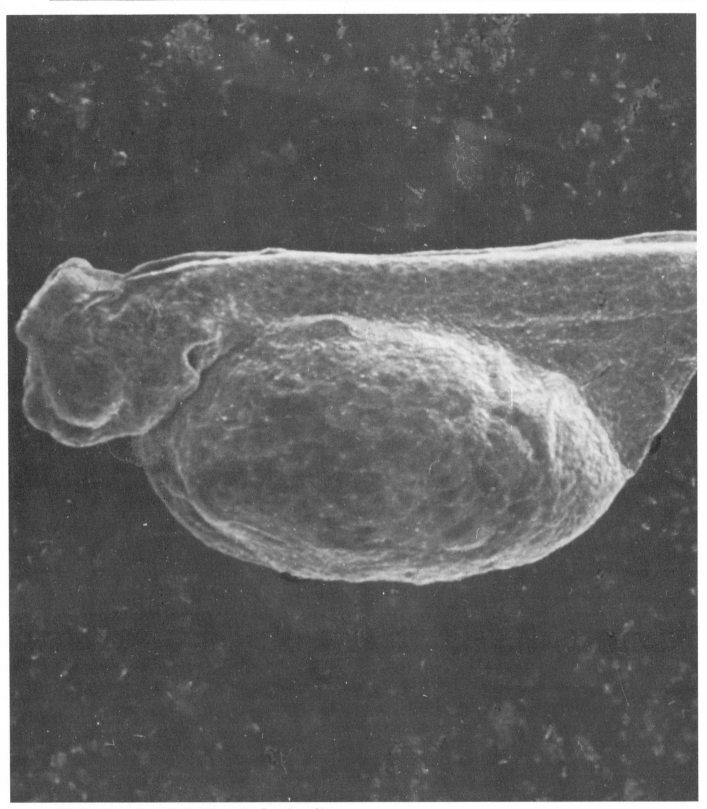

This is what a discus looks like on the first day of its hatching. The large belly is full of egg yolk, which provides nourishment for the fry before the ingestion/digestion system is completely developed. The closeup on the facing page shows the head in detail, with the cement glands and the developing eye. Photos by Dr. Harry Grier.

The Most Famous Fish Breeder

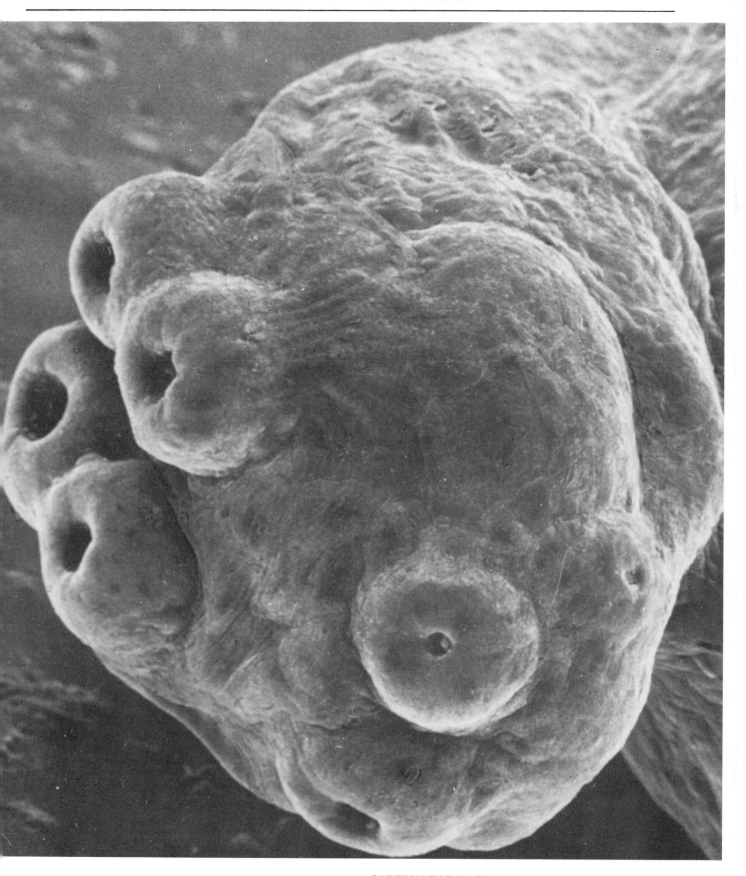

CAPTION FOR PAGE 112
A pair of Wattley's turquoise discus. Photo by Dr.
Herbert R. Axelrod.